To Jolene, from the staff and he
friends at Uhlich Childrens Home

July 9. 1976-

THE ILLUSTRATED WORLD OF THOREAU

Nature will bear the closest inspection.
She invites us to lay our eyes level
with her smallest leaf, and take an
insect view of its plain.

A field of water betrays the spirit that
is in the air. It has new life and motion.
It is intermediate between land and sky.

On land, only the grass and trees wave,
but the water itself is rippled by the wind.
I see the breeze dash over it in
streaks and flakes of light.

THE ILLUSTRATED WORLD OF THOREAU

Words by Henry David Thoreau
Photographs by Ivan Massar

Edited by Howard Chapnick

With an Afterword by
Loren Eiseley

GROSSET & DUNLAP
Publishers • New York

Published Simultaneously in Canada

Library of Congress Catalog Card Number: 73-15134

ISBN: 0-448-01028-3

First Printing

Printed in the United States of America

A BLACK STAR BOOK

Designed by Robert S. Nemser, Nemser and Howard, Inc.

To Jeanette
H.C.

For Barbara, Andrea and David
I.M.

Our thanks to Claire Bazinet for her editorial commitment,
concern and search for perfection;

And to Kay Lee for her creative design concept.

First daguerreotype taken of Thoreau printed with the permission and through the courtesy of the National Portrait Gallery, Washington, D.C., Smithsonian Institution.

Henry David Thoreau, the iconoclastic transcendentalist philosopher and essayist, was one of the first American ecologists to be sensitive to the impact of the Industrial Revolution on man and his surroundings. Through troubled eyes he saw the tragedy of man possessed by his possessions, the seemingly wealthy forging their own "golden or silver fetters" with their "accumulated dross." He cried out for "Simplicity, simplicity, simplicity!"—urging man to follow the lessons of nature and spurn the seductive marvels of the new technology. Only now, a century later, is Thoreau's cry beginning to be heard.

In recent years young and old alike, "Marching to the step of a different drummer," have come to question the materialistic values of their societies. Some, unsatisfied, have dropped out of society, experimenting with mind-expanding drugs or exploring Eastern religions in a vain search for meaning in the absurdities of the Nuclear Age. But many have turned to Thoreau to find inspiration in his celebration of nature and peace in its grand design. Accepting Thoreau's invitation to inspect the smallest leaf has released many men from a harried existence in which they have observed without seeing and touched without feeling.

Following this lead, man has slowly awakened from his neo-romance with technology, only to be confronted by its ravages. The first tentative steps toward restoring the fine, life-sustaining balance between man and his environment have now been taken. The struggle promises to be long and hard, and time is short.

A century ago, Thoreau's enlightened view also included man's social institutions. He spoke out against slavery and the machine's depredations on labor. He was concerned with the individual's obligation to his own conscience and the myth of government infallibility. Only now do his whispers reach our ears.

Thoreau, a private man, alone but not lonely, has willed us via his writings a deep, enduring insight into the inseparable relationships of man, society, and nature. Can we afford not to listen?

Howard Chapnick

HENRY

Thoreau laid out Bedford Street when he was a surveyor. We live on his terrain. I could see his gravesite across the street from my window if the trees were not between us.

I have always liked the simplicity of Thoreau's gravestone. The family plot rests on a knoll in Sleepy Hollow Cemetery. The Thoreau family gravestone lists the names of John and Cynthia D. Thoreau followed by their four children. Small individual stones for FATHER, MOTHER, and each child surround the larger marker. There's HENRY off in a corner just like the other kids. His simple name stone stands quietly like a plant in a garden of names, with no recognition that this man was *Henry David Thoreau*. He has merely equal billing. He would have liked that, I believe. I am reminded of the human dimensions of his life—what he considered important in contrast to what his fellow townspeople considered important.

I read *Walden* in the navy at the age of eighteen. The first act of my life that I can attribute to Thoreau's influence is my going over the hill while in the navy. Having been "decorated" with six battle stars, I became a pacifist. It was the first time I had dared to question anything that was universally considered right.

Since then, I have felt a kindred spirit linking Thoreau's written journals and my photographic journeys. Thoreau's journals focus upon a narrow geographic range of Concord and elsewhere in New England. But his influence has rippled out into the world. My journeys have taken me into and around the world, but always with a desire to focus and simplify, because I have learned from Thoreau how far I can travel by enjoying what is underfoot. I have applied Thoreau's precepts in my photography by slowing down, taking a closer look, and learning to *see*. I have learned that a good picture is a simple picture: one undiluted statement rather than a glimpse of everything. While wandering with the camera, or selecting for this book from photographs already taken, a potential picture would appeal to me because I would think, There's something that would capture Thoreau's appreciation or arouse his disdain; I would love to show that to him for his response. I attempted to look for things that he would find the need to comment on. At times I felt as if I were seeing for him.

Ivan Massar

CONTENTS

Morning Brings Back the Heroic Ages	2
Lives of Quiet Desperation	8
Live Simply and Wisely	16
Man, the Machine	20
Snow Stars	24
And No Place to Sit	30
A Land of Faery	34
That Wonderful Frostwork	38
The Frost Comes Out of Me	42
Spring Rain	50
Seize Time by the Forelock	58
To What End?	70
I Hate Museums	76
Walk Silent and Seeing	82
Now Is Nature's Grandest Voice Heard	88
A Temple Called the Body	90
Clothing	98
Now Mottled Hues Clothe the Earth	104
Old Age	106
All Change Is a Miracle to Contemplate	110
Sweet Sylvia!	114
The Silent Poor	116

Like Oxen in a Flower Garden 118
Civil Disobedience 124
The Mists Brood Over Me 136
Eternal Walden 138
To See the Spring Come In 154
I Left the Woods 160
A Different Drummer 162
Thoreau's Vision of the Natural World *by Loren Eiseley* 164

from *Walden: or, Life in the Woods,* 1854

from Thoreau's journals, 1834–1862

from *On the Duty of Civil Disobedience,* 1848

THE ILLUSTRATED WORLD OF THOREAU

Morning Brings Back the Heroic Ages

Every morning was a cheerful invitation to make my life of equal simplicity, and I may say innocence, with Nature herself. I have been as sincere a worshiper of Aurora as the Greeks. I got up early and bathed in the pond; that was a religious exercise, and one of the best things which I did. They say that characters were engraven on the bathing tub of King Tching-thang to this effect: "Renew thyself completely each day; do it again, and again, and forever again." I can understand that. Morning brings back the heroic ages. I was as much affected by the faint hum of a mosquito making its invisible and unimaginable tour through my apartment at earliest dawn, when I was sitting with door and windows open, as I could be by any trumpet that ever sang of fame. It was Homer's requiem; itself an Iliad and Odyssey in the air, singing its own wrath and wanderings. There was something cosmical about it; a standing advertisement, till forbidden, of the everlasting vigor and fertility of the world. The morning, which is the most memorable season of the day, is the awakening hour. Then there is least somnolence in us; and for an hour, at least, some part of us awakes which slumbers all the rest of the day and night. Little is to be expected of that day, if it can be called a day, to which we are not awakened by our Genius, but by the mechanical nudgings of some servitor, are not awakened by our own newly acquired force and aspirations from within, accompanied by the undulations of celestial music, instead of factory bells, and a fragrance filling the air—to a higher life than we fell asleep from; and thus the darkness bear its fruit, and prove itself to be good, no less than the light. That man who does not believe that each day contains an earlier, more sacred and auroral hour than he has yet profaned, has despaired of life, and is pursuing a descending and darkening way. After a partial cessation of his sensuous life, the soul of man, or its organs rather, are reinvigorated each day, and his Genius tries again what noble life it can make. All memorable events, I should say, transpire in morning time and in a morning atmosphere.

To him whose elastic and vigorous thought keeps pace with the sun, the day is a perpetual morning. It matters not what the clocks say or the attitudes and labors of men. Morning is when I am awake and there is a dawn in me.

We must learn to reawaken and keep ourselves awake, not by mechanical aids, but by an infinite expectation of the dawn, which does not forsake us in our soundest sleep. I know of no more encouraging fact than the unquestionable ability of man to elevate his life by a conscious endeavor. It is something to be able to paint a particular picture, or to carve a statue, and so to make a few objects beautiful; but it is far more glorious to carve and paint the very atmosphere and medium through which we look, which morally we can do. To affect the quality of the day, that is the highest of arts. Every man is tasked to make his life, even in its details, worthy of the contemplation of his most elevated and critical hour. If we refused, or rather used up, such paltry information as we get, the oracles would distinctly inform us how this might be done.

WORK SAFE

Lives of Quiet Desperation

The mass of men lead lives of quiet desperation. What is called resignation is confirmed desperation. From the desperate city you go into the desperate country, and have to console yourself with the bravery of minks and muskrats. A stereotyped but unconscious despair is concealed even under what are called the games and amusements of mankind. There is no play in them, for this comes after work. But it is a characteristic of wisdom not to do desperate things.

When we consider what, to use the words of the catechism, is the chief end of man, and what are the true necessaries and means of life, it appears as if men had deliberately chosen the common mode of living because they preferred it to any other. Yet they honestly think there is no choice left. But alert and healthy natures remember that the sun rose clear. It is never too late to give up our prejudices. No way of thinking or doing, however ancient, can be trusted without proof. What everybody echoes or in silence passes by as true today may turn out to be falsehood tomorrow, mere smoke of opinion, which some had trusted for a cloud that would sprinkle fertilizing rain on their fields. What old people say you cannot do you try and find that you can. Old deeds for old people, and new deeds for new.

B&O
B&O
B&O
B&O
B&O

B&O
B&O

Live Simply and Wisely

I am convinced, both by faith and experience, that to maintain one's self on this earth is not a hardship but a pastime, if we will live simply and wisely; as the pursuits of the simpler nations are still the sports of the more artificial. It is not necessary that a man should earn his living by the sweat of his brow, unless he sweats easier than I do.

One young man of my acquaintance, who has inherited some acres, told me that he thought he should live as I did, *if he had the means.* I would not have anyone adopt *my* mode of living on any account; for, besides that before he has fairly learned it I may have found out another for myself, I desire that there may be as many different persons in the world as possible; but I would have each one be very careful to find out and pursue *his own* way, and not his father's or his mother's or his neighbor's instead. The youth may build or plant or sail, only let him not be hindered from doing that which he tells me he would like to do. It is by a mathematical point only that we are wise, as the sailor or the fugitive slave keeps the polestar in his eye; but that is sufficient guidance for all our life. We may not arrive at our port within a calculable period, but we would preserve the true course.

Still we live meanly, like ants; though the fable tells us that we were long ago changed into men; like pygmies we fight with cranes; it is error upon error, and clout upon clout, and our best virtue has for its occasion a superfluous and evitable wretchedness. Our life is frittered away by detail. An honest man has hardly need to count more than his ten fingers, or in extreme cases he may add his ten toes, and lump the rest. Simplicity, simplicity, simplicity! I say, let your affairs be as two or three, and not a hundred or a thousand; instead of a million count half a dozen, and keep your accounts on your thumb nail. In the midst of this chopping sea of civilized life, such are the clouds and storms and quicksands and thousand-and-one items to be allowed for, that a man has to live, if he would not founder and go to the bottom and not make his port at all, by dead reckoning, and he must be a great calculator indeed who succeeds. Simplify, simplify. Instead of three meals a day, if it be necessary eat but one; instead of a hundred dishes, five; and reduce other things in proportion.

Man, the Machine

Most men, even in this comparatively free country, through mere ignorance and mistake, are so occupied with the factitious cares and superfluously coarse labors of life that its finer fruits cannot be plucked by them. Their fingers, from excessive toil, are too clumsy and tremble too much for that. Actually, the laboring man has not leisure for a true integrity day by day; he cannot afford to sustain the manliest relations to men; his labor would be depreciated in the market. He has no time to be anything but a machine. How can he remember well his ignorance—which his growth requires—who has so often to use his knowledge? We should feed and clothe him gratuitously sometimes, and recruit him with our cordials, before we judge of him. The finest qualities of our nature, like the bloom on fruits, can be preserved only by the most delicate handling. Yet we do not treat ourselves nor one another thus tenderly.

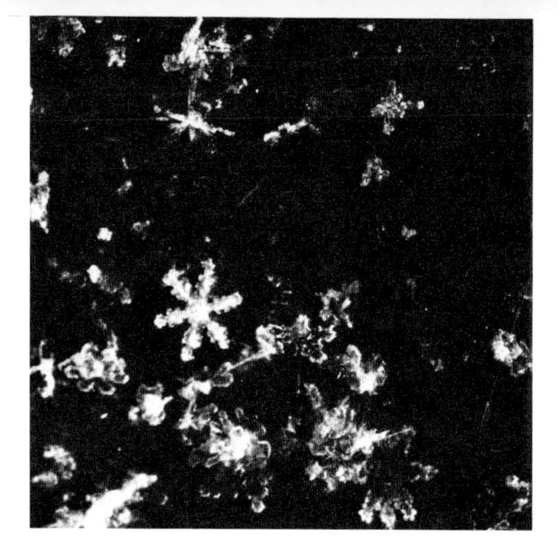

Snow Stars

The thin snow now driving from the north and lodging on my coat consists of those beautiful star crystals, not cottony and chubby spokes, as on the 13th December, but thin and partly transparent crystals. They are about a tenth of an inch in diameter, perfect little wheels with six spokes without a tire, or rather with six perfect little leafets, fernlike, with a distinct straight and slender midrib, raying from the centre. . . . How full of the creative genius is the air in which these are generated! I should hardly admire more if real stars fell and lodged on my coat. Nature is full of genius, full of the divinity; so that not a snowflake escapes its fashioning hand. Nothing is cheap and coarse, neither dewdrops nor snowflakes. Soon the storm increases—it was already very severe to face—and the snow comes finer, more white and powdery. Who knows but this is the original form of all snowflakes, but that when I observe these crystal stars falling around me they are but just generated in the low mist next the earth?

A divinity must have stirred within them before the crystals did thus shoot and set. Wheels of the storm-chariots. The same law that shapes the earth-star shapes the snow-star. As surely as the petals of a flower are fixed, each of these countless snow-stars comes whirling to earth, pronouncing thus, with emphasis, the number six.

What a world we live in! where myriads of these little disks, so beautiful to the most prying eye, are whirled down on every traveller's coat, the observant and the unobservant, and on the restless squirrel's fur, and on the far-stretching fields and forests, the wooded dells, and the mountaintops. Far, far away from the haunts of man, they roll down some little slope, fall over and come to their bearings, and melt or lose their beauty in the mass, ready anon to swell some little rill with their contribution, and so, at last, the universal ocean from which they came. There they lie, like the wreck of chariot wheels after a battle in the skies. Meanwhile the meadow mouse shoves them aside in his gallery, the schoolboy casts them in his snowball, or the woodman's sled glides smoothly over them, these glorious spangles, the sweeping of heaven's floor. And they all sing, melting as they sing of the mysteries of the number six—six, six, six. He takes up the water of the sea in his hand, leaving the salt; He disperses it in mist through the skies; He recollects and sprinkles it like grain in six-rayed snowy stars over the earth, there to lie till He dissolves its bonds again.

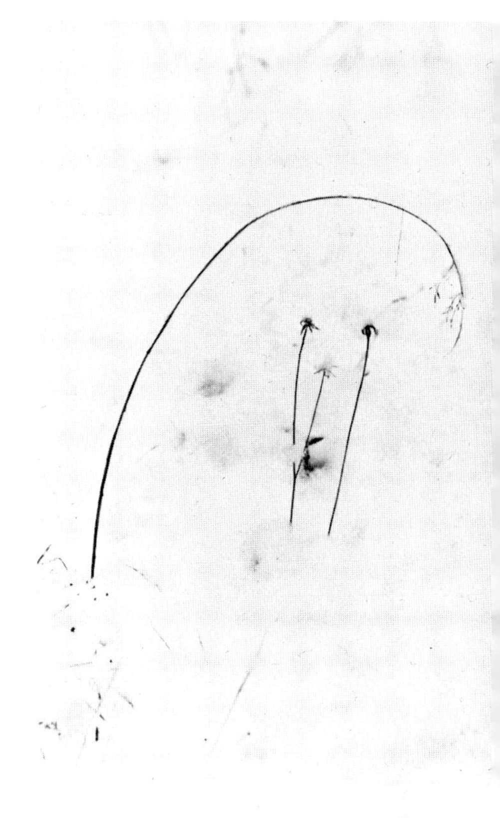

And No Place to Sit

The sky appears broader now than it did. The day has opened its eyelids wider. . . .

Everywhere snow, gathered into sloping drifts about the walls and fences, and, beneath the snow, the frozen ground, and men are compelled to deposit the summer's provision in burrows in the earth like the ground squirrel. Many creatures, daunted by the prospect, migrated in the fall, but man remains and walks over the frozen snowcrust and over the stiffened rivers and ponds, and draws now upon his summer stores. Life is reduced to its lowest terms. There is no home for you now, in this freezing wind, but in that shelter which you prepared in the summer. You steer straight across the fields to that in season. I can with difficulty tell when I am over the river. There is a similar crust over my heart. Where I rambled in the summer and gathered flowers and rested on the grass by the brookside in the shade, now no grass nor flowers, no brook nor shade, but cold, unvaried snow, stretching mile after mile, and no place to sit.

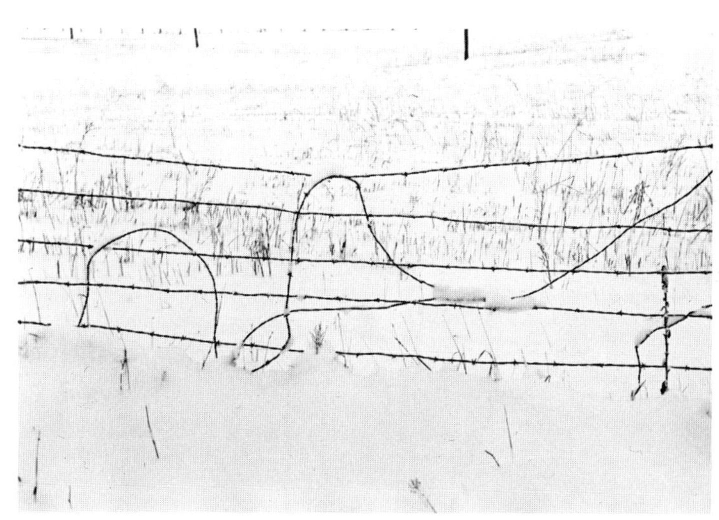

A Land of Faery

This morning we have something between ice and frost on the trees, etc. The whole earth, as last night, but much more, is encased in ice, which on the plowed fields makes a singular icy coat a quarter of an inch or more in thickness. About 9 o'clock A.M., I go to Lee's *via* Hubbard's Wood and Holden's Swamp and the riverside, for the middle is open. The stones and cow dung, and the walls too, are all cased in ice on the north side. The latter look like alum rocks. This, not frozen mist or frost, but frozen drizzle, collected around the slightest cores, gives prominence to the least withered herbs and grasses. Where yesterday was a plain, smooth field, appears now a teeming crop of fat, *icy* herbage. The stems of the herbs on their north sides are enlarged from ten to a hundred times. The addition is so universally on the north side that a traveller could not lose the points of compass today, though it should [be] never so dark, for every blade of grass would serve to guide him, telling from which side the storm came yesterday. These straight stems of grasses stand up like white batons or sceptres, and make conspicuous foreground to the landscape, from six inches to three feet high. C. thought that these fat, icy branches on the withered grass and herbs had no nucleus, but looking closer I showed him the fine black wiry threads on which they impinged, which made him laugh with surprise. The very cow dung is incrusted, and the clover and sorrel send up a dull green gleam through their icy coat, like strange plants. The pebbles in the plowed land are seen as through a transparent coating of gum. Some weeds bear the ice in masses, some, like the trumpetweed and tansy, in balls for each dried flower. What a crash of jewels as you walk! The most careless walker, who never deigned to look at these humble weeds before, cannot help observing them now.

This is why the herbage is left to stand dry in the fields all winter. Upon a solid foundation of ice stand out, pointing in all directions between northwest and northeast, or within the limits of ninety degrees, little spicula or crystallized points, half an inch or more in length.

I have now passed the bars and am approaching the Cliffs. The forms and variety of the ice are particularly rich here, there are so many low bushes and weeds before me as I ascend toward the sun, especially very small white pines almost merged in the ice-incrusted ground. All objects, even the apple trees and rails, are to the eye polished silver. It is a perfect land of faery. As if the world were a great frosted cake with its ornaments. The boughs gleam like silver candlesticks. Le Jeune describes the same in Canada, in 1636, as *"nos grands bois ne paroissoient qu'une forest de cristal."* The silvery ice stands out an inch by three fourths [of] an inch in width on the north side of every twig of these apple trees, with rich irregularities of its own in its edge. When I stoop and examine some fat icy stubble in my path, I find for all core a ridiculous wiry russet thread, scarce visible, not a hundredth part its size, which breaks with the ice under my feet; yet where this has a minute stub of a branch only a fortieth of an inch in length, there is a corresponding clumsy icy protuberance on the surface an eighth of an inch off. Nature works with such luxuriance and fury that she follows the least hint. And on the twigs of bushes, for each bud there is a corresponding icy swelling.

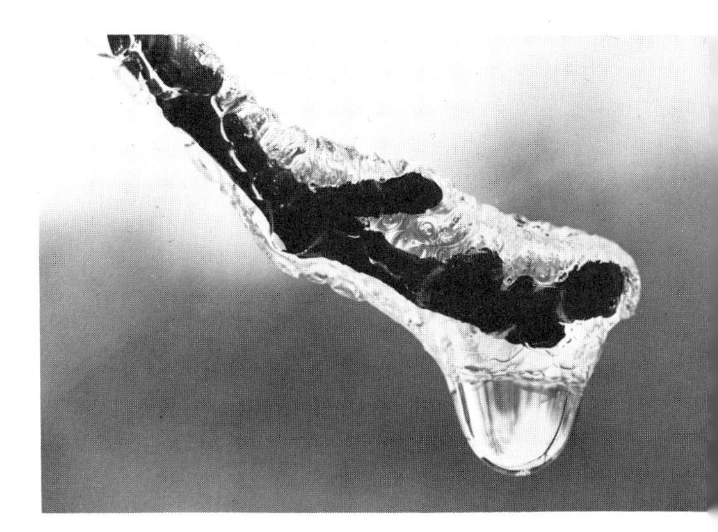

That Wonderful Frostwork

That wonderful frostwork of the 13th and 14th was too rare to be neglected—succeeded as it was, also, by two days of glaze—but, having company, I lost half the advantage of it. It was remarkable to have a fog for four days in midwinter without wind. We had just had sudden severe cold weather, and I suspect that the fog was occasioned by a warmer air, probably from the sea, coming into contact with our cold ice-and-snow-clad earth. The hoar frost formed of the fog was such a one as I do not remember on such a scale. Apparently as the fog was coarser and far more abundant, it was whiter, less delicate to examine, and of far greater depth than a frostwork formed of dew. We did not have an opportunity to see how it would look in the sun, but seen against the mist or fog it was too fair to be remembered.

Perhaps the most unusual thing about this phenomenon was its duration. The air seemed almost perfectly still the first day, and I did not perceive that the frosting lost anything; nay, it evidently grew during the first half of the day at least, for it was cold at the same time that it was foggy.

Everyone, no doubt, has looked with delight, holding his face low, at that beautiful frostwork which so frequently in winter mornings is seen bristling about the throat of every breathing hole in the earth's surface. In this case the fog, the earth's breath made visible, was in such abundance that it invested all our vales and hills, and the frostwork, accordingly, instead of being confined to the chinks and crannies of the earth, covered the mightiest trees, so that we, walking beneath them, had the same wonderful prospect and environment that an insect would have in the former case. We, going along our roads, had such a prospect as an insect would have making its way through a chink in the earth which was bristling with hoar frost.

That glaze! I know what it was by my own experience; it was the frozen breath of the earth upon its beard.

Take the most rigid tree, the whole effect is peculiarly soft and spiritlike, for there is no marked edge or outline. How could you draw the outline of these snowy fingers seen against the fog, without exaggeration? There is no more a boundary line or circumference that can be drawn, than a diameter. Hardly could the New England farmer drive to market under these trees without feeling that his sense of beauty was addressed. He would be aware that the phenomenon called beauty was become visible, if one were at leisure or had had the right culture to appreciate it.

Many times I thought that if the particular tree, commonly an elm, under which I was walking or riding were the only one like it in the country, it would [be] worth a journey across the continent to see it. Indeed, I have no doubt that such journeys would be undertaken on hearing a true account of it. But, instead of being confined to a single tree, this wonder was as cheap and common as the air itself. Every man's woodlot was a miracle and surprise to him, and for those who could not go so far there were the trees in the street and the weeds in the yard. It was much like (in effect) that snow that lodges on the fine dead twigs on the lower part of a pine wood, resting there in the twilight commonly only till it has done snowing and the wind arises. But in this case it did not rest *on* the twig, but grew out from it horizontally, and it was not confined to the lowest twigs, but covered the whole forest and every surface.

Looking down the street, you might say that the scene differed from the ordinary one as frosted cake differs from plain bread. In some moods you might suspect that it was the work of enchantment. Some magician had put your village into a crucible and it had crystallized thus.

The Frost Comes Out of Me

It is a genial and reassuring day; the mere warmth of the west wind amounts almost to balminess. The softness of the air mollifies our own dry and congealed substance. I sit down by a wall to see if I can muse again. We become, as it were, pliant and ductile again to strange but memorable influences; we are led a little way by our genius. We are affected like the earth, and yield to the elemental tenderness; winter breaks up within us; the frost is coming out of me, and I am heaved like the road; accumulated masses of ice and snow dissolve, and thoughts like a freshet pour down unwonted channels. A strain of music comes to solace the traveller over earth's downs and dignify his chagrins, the petty men whom he meets are the shadows of grander to come.

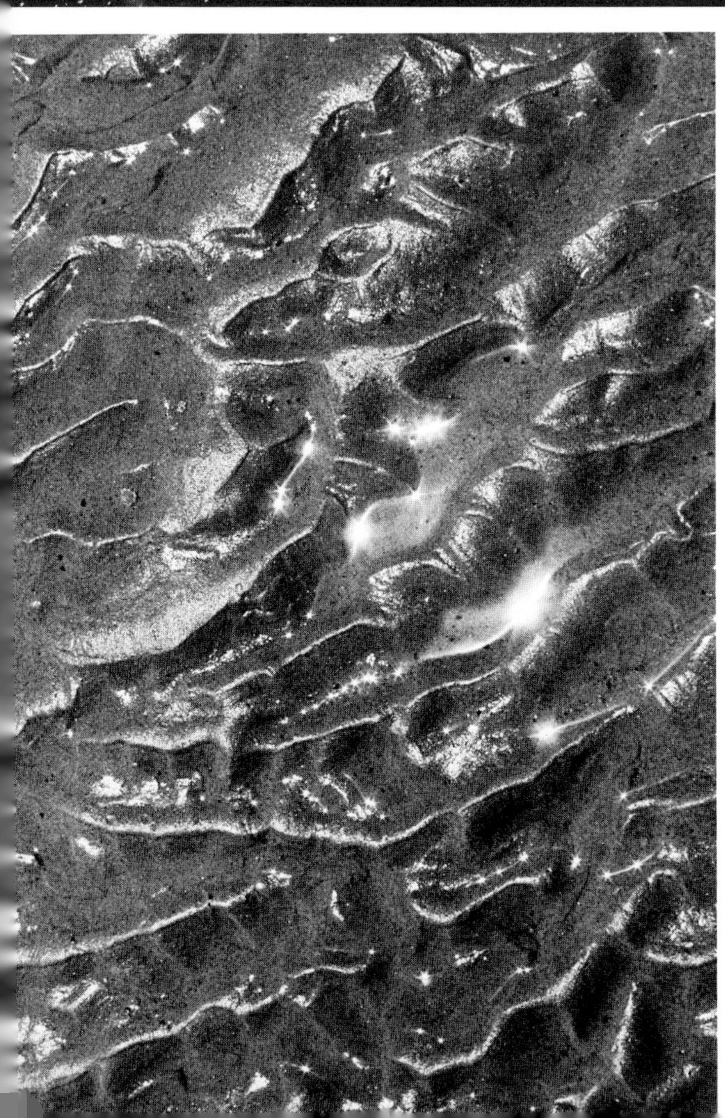

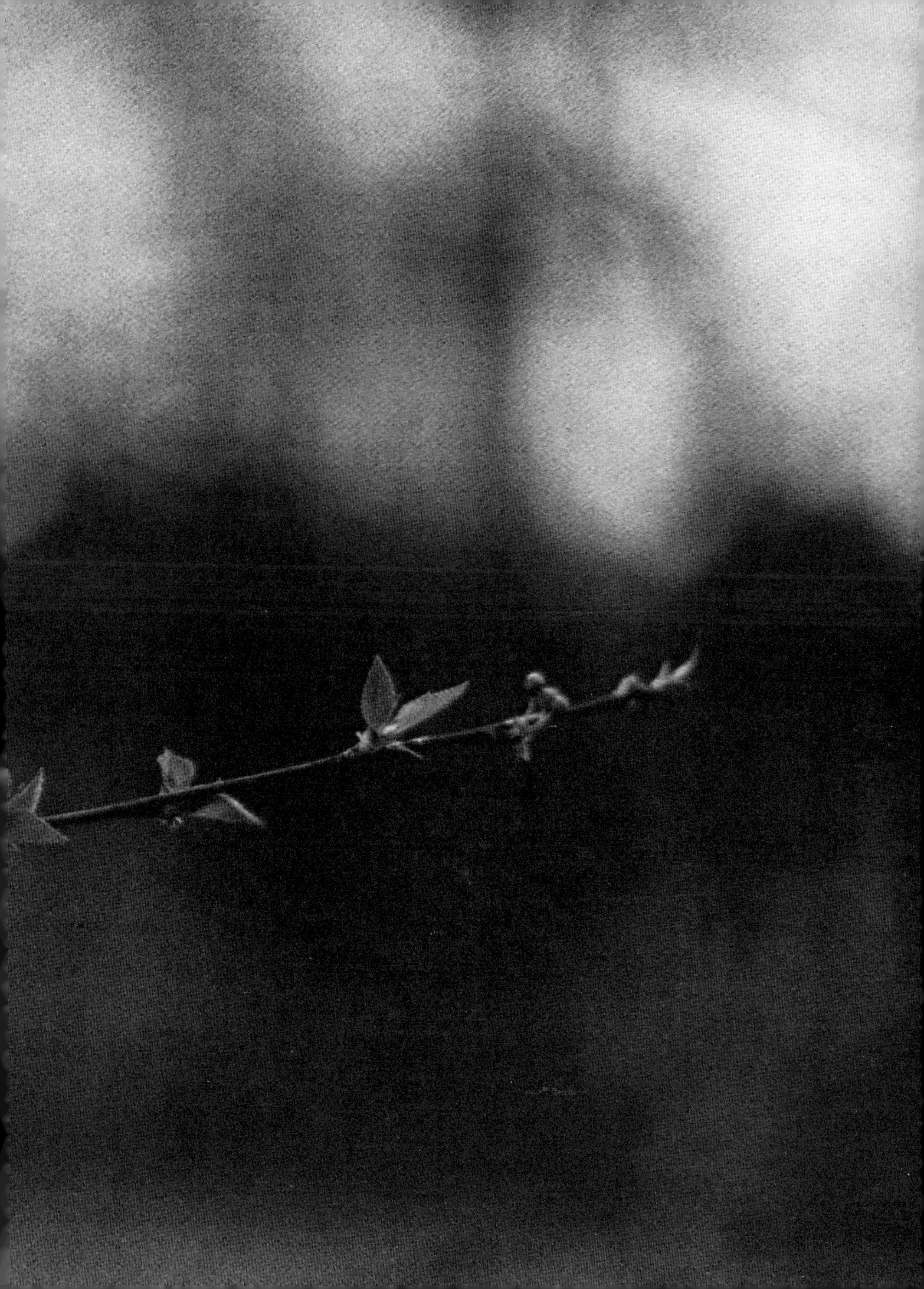

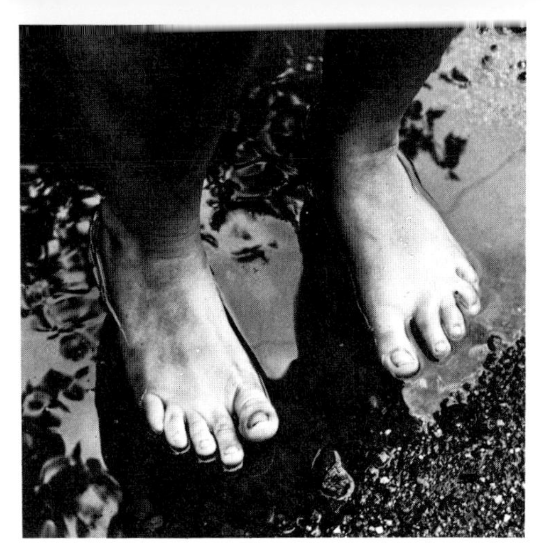

Spring Rain

It is so mild and moist as I saunter along by the wall east of the Hill that I remember, or anticipate, one of those warm rainstorms in the spring, when the earth is just laid bare, the wind is south, and the cladonia lichens are swollen and lusty with moisture, your foot sinking into them and pressing the water out as from a sponge, and the sandy places also are drinking it in. You wander indefinitely in a beaded coat, wet to the skin of your legs, sit on moss-clad rocks and stumps, and hear the lisping of migrating sparrows flitting amid the shrub oaks, sit long at a time, still, and have your thoughts. A rain which is as serene as fair weather, suggesting fairer weather than was ever seen. You could hug the clods that defile you. You feel the fertilizing influence of the rain in your mind. The part of you that is wettest is fullest of life, like the lichens. You discover evidences of immortality not known to divines. You cease to die. You detect some buds and sprouts of life. Every step in the old rye-field is on virgin soil.

And then the rain comes thicker and faster than before, thawing the remaining frost in the ground, detaining the migrating bird; and you turn your back to it, full of serene, contented thought, soothed by the steady dropping on the withered leaves, more at home for being abroad, more comfortable for being wet, sinking at each step deep into the thawing earth, gladly breaking through the gray rotting ice. The dullest sounds seem sweetly modulated by the air. You leave your tracks in fields of spring rye, scaring the fox-colored sparrows along the woodsides. You cannot go home yet; you stay and sit in the rain. You glide along the distant woodside, full of joy and expectation, seeing nothing but beauty, hearing nothing but music, as free as the fox-colored sparrow, seeing far ahead, a courageous knight, a great philosopher, not indebted to any academy or college for this expansion, but chiefly to the April rain, which descendeth on all alike.

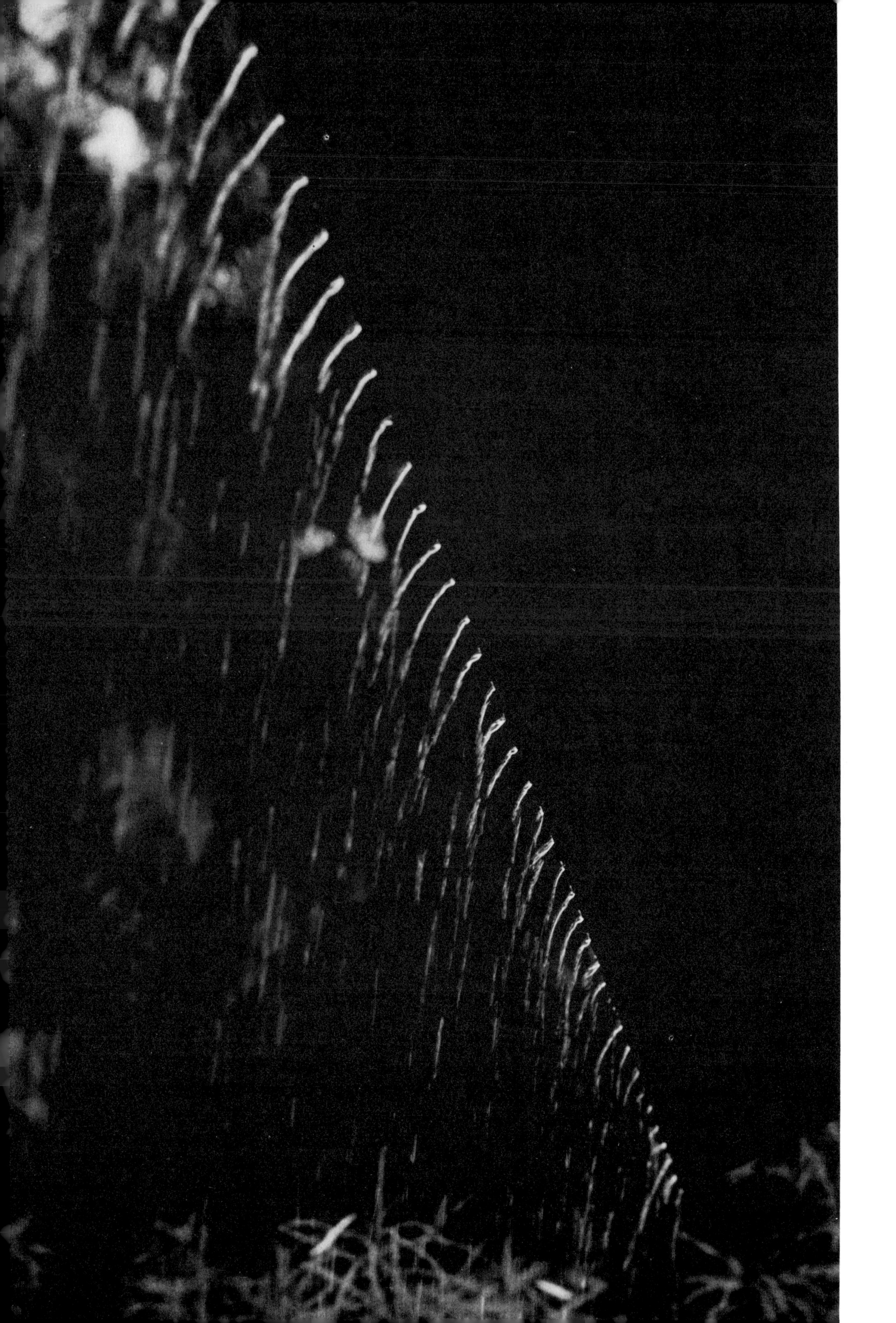

Seize Time by the Forelock

There is a season for everything, and we do not notice a given phenomenon except at that season, if, indeed, it can be called the same phenomenon at any other season.

There is a time to watch the ripples on Ripple Lake, to look for arrowheads, to study the rocks and lichens, a time to walk on sandy deserts; and the observer of nature must improve these seasons as much as the farmer his. So boys fly kites and play ball or hawkie at particular times all over the State. A wise man will know what game to play today, and play it. We must not be governed by rigid rules, as by the almanac, but let the season rule us. The moods and thoughts of man are revolving just as steadily and incessantly as nature's. Nothing must be postponed.

GRILLED CHEESE
BACON-LETTUCE-TOM.
HOT PASTROMI
HOT DOGS STEAMED OR GRILLED
ENGLISH MUFFINS
SANDWICHES
R SALAMI

BLACK AND WHITE 1.00
THE CURRENT ADMINISTRATION
GOOD CLEAN FUN
ATIVES

Take time by the forelock. Now or never! You must live in the present, launch yourself on every wave, find your eternity in each moment. Fools stand on their island opportunities and look toward another land. There is no other land; there is no other life but this, or the like of this. Where the good husbandman is, there is the good soil. Take any other course, and life will be a succession of regrets. Let us see vessels sailing prosperously before the wind, and not simply stranded barks. There is no world for the penitent and regretful.

To What End?

To what end, pray, is so much stone hammered? In Arcadia, when I was there, I did not see any hammering stone. Nations are possessed with an insane ambition to perpetuate the memory of themselves by the amount of hammered stone they leave. What if equal pains were taken to smooth and polish their manners? One piece of good sense would be more memorable than a monument as high as the moon. I love better to see stones in place. The grandeur of Thebes was a vulgar grandeur. More sensible is a rod of stone wall that bounds an honest man's field than a hundred-gated Thebes that has wandered farther from the true end of life. The religion and civilization which are barbaric and heathenish build splendid temples; but what you might call Christianity does not. Most of the stone a nation hammers goes toward its tomb only. It buries itself alive. As for the Pyramids, there is nothing to wonder at in them so much as the fact that so many men could be found degraded enough to spend their lives constructing a tomb for some ambitious booby, whom it would have been wiser and manlier to have drowned in the Nile, and then given his body to the dogs. I might possibly invent some excuse for them and him, but I have no time for it. As for the religion and love of art of the builders, it is much the same all the world over, whether the building be an Egyptian temple or the United States Bank. It costs more than it comes to. The mainspring is vanity, assisted by the love of garlic and bread and butter.

BUILDINGS

THOU SHALT LOVE THE LORD THY GOD
ואהבת את יהוה אלהיך

I Hate Museums

I hate museums; there is nothing so weighs upon my spirits. They are the catacombs of nature. One green bud of spring, one willow catkin, one faint trill from a migrating sparrow would set the world on its legs again. The life that is in a single green weed is of more worth than all this death. They are dead nature collected by dead men. I know not whether I muse most at the bodies stuffed with cotton and sawdust or those stuffed with bowels and fleshy fibre outside the cases.

Where is the proper herbarium, the true cabinet of shells, and museum of skeletons, but in the meadow where the flower bloomed, by the seaside where the tide cast up the fish, and on the hills and in the valleys where the beast laid down its life and the skeleton of the traveller reposes on the grass? What right have mortals to parade these things on their legs again, with their wires, and, when heaven has decreed that they shall return to dust again, to return them to sawdust? Would you have a dried specimen of a world, or a pickled one?

Embalming is a sin against heaven and earth—against heaven, who has recalled the soul and set free the servile elements, and against the earth, which is thus robbed of her dust. I have had my right-perceiving senses so disturbed in these haunts as to mistake a veritable living man for a stuffed specimen, and surveyed him with dumb wonder as the strangest of the whole collection. For the strangest is that which, being in many particulars most like, is in some essential particular most unlike.

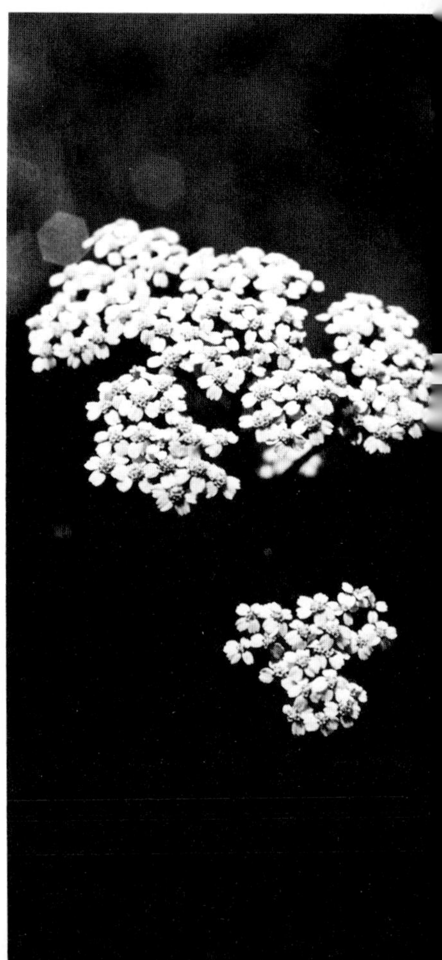

Walk Silent and Seeing

Each phase of nature, while not invisible, is yet not too distinct and obtrusive. It is there to be found when we look for it, but not demanding our attention. It is like a silent but sympathizing companion in whose company we retain most of the advantages of solitude, with whom we can walk and talk, or be silent, naturally, without the necessity of talking in a strain foreign to the place.

I know of but one or two persons with whom I can afford to walk. With most the walk degenerates into a mere vigorous use of your legs, ludicrously purposeless, while you are discussing some mighty argument, each one having his say, spoiling each other's day, worrying one another with conversation, hustling one another with our conversation. I know of no use in the walking part in this case, except that we may seem to be getting on together toward some goal; but of course we keep our original distance all the way. Jumping every wall and ditch with vigor in the vain hope of shaking your companion off. Trying to kill two birds with one stone, though they sit at opposite points of [the] compass, to see nature and do the honors to one who does not.

Now Is Nature's Grandest Voice Heard

I hear it in midafternoon, muttering,
crashing in the muggy air in mid heaven,
a little south of the village as I go through
it, like the tumbling down of piles of
boards, and get a few sprinkles in the sun.
Nature has found her hoarse summer voice
again, like the lowing of a cow let out
to pasture. It is Nature's rutting season.
Even as the birds sing tumultuously and
glance by with fresh and brilliant plumage,
so now is Nature's grandest voice heard,
and her sharpest flashes seen. The air has
resumed its voice, and the lightning, like
a yellow spring flower, illumines the dark
banks of the clouds. All the pregnant
earth is bursting into life like a mildew,
accompanied with noise and fire and
tumult. Some oestrus stings her that she
dashes headlong against the steeples and
bellows hollowly, making the earth
tremble. She comes dropping rain like
a cow with overflowing udder. The winds
drive her; the dry fields milk her. It is
the familiar note of another warbler,
just arrived, echoing amid the roofs.

A Temple Called the Body

Every man is the builder of a temple, called his body, to the god he worships, after a style purely his own, nor can he get off by hammering marble instead. We are all sculptors and painters, and our material is our own flesh and blood and bones. Any nobleness begins at once to refine a man's features, any meanness or sensuality to imbrute them.

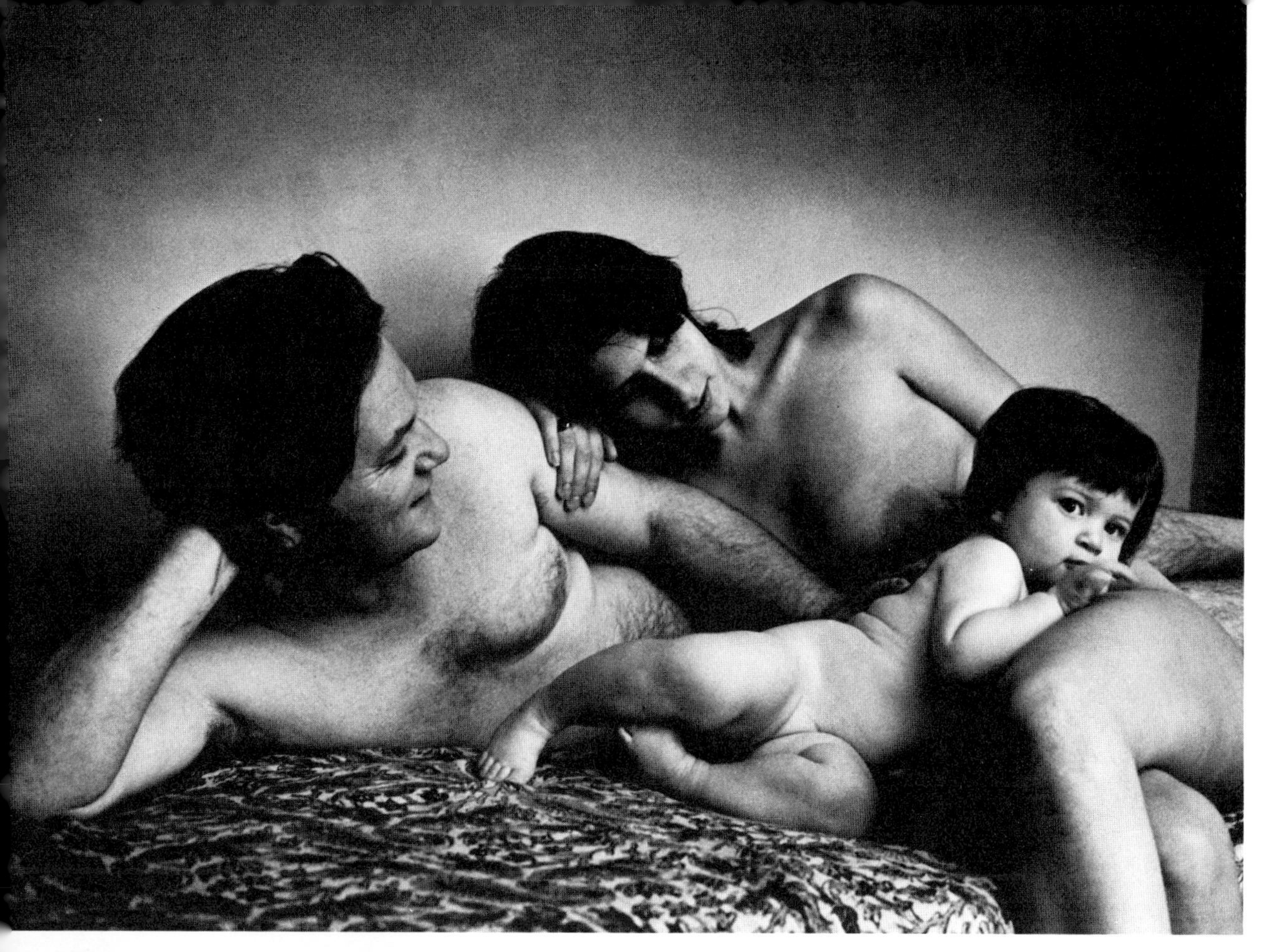

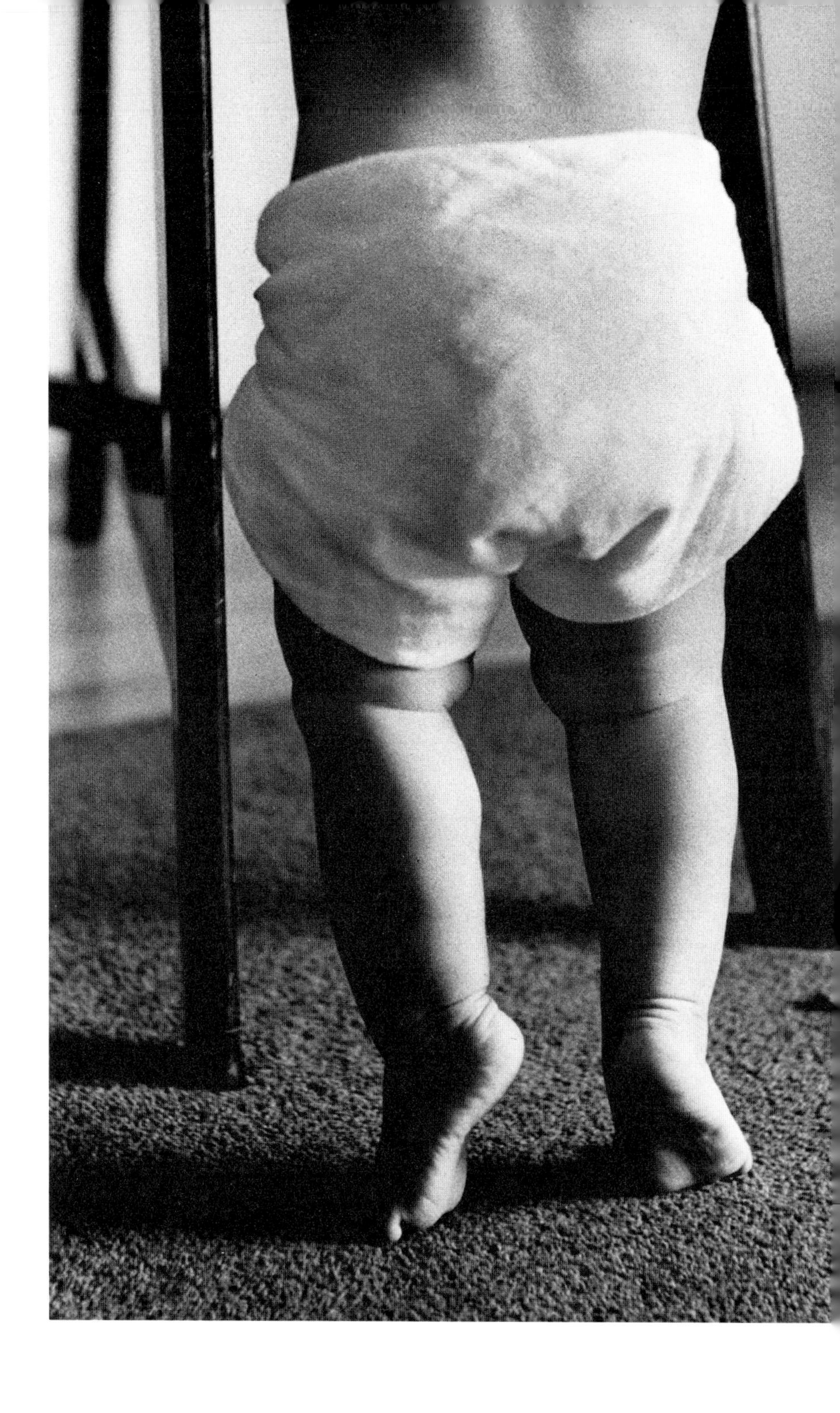

Clothing

As for Clothing, to come at once to the practical part of the question, perhaps we are led oftener by the love of novelty and a regard for the opinions of men, in procuring it, than by a true utility. Let him who has work to do recollect that the object of clothing is, first, to retain the vital heat, and secondly, in this state of society, to cover nakedness, and he may judge how much of any necessary or important work may be accomplished without adding to his wardrobe. Kings and queens who wear a suit but once, though made by some tailor or dressmaker to their majesties, cannot know the comfort of wearing a suit that fits. They are no better than wooden horses to hang the clean clothes on. Every day our garments become more assimilated to ourselves, receiving the impress of the wearer's character, until we hesitate to lay them aside, without such delay and medical appliances and some such solemnity even as our bodies. No man ever stood the lower in my estimation for having a patch in his clothes; yet I am sure that there is greater anxiety, commonly, to have fashionable, or at least clean and unpatched clothes, than to have a sound conscience. But even if the rent is not mended, perhaps the worst vice betrayed is improvidence. I sometimes try my acquaintances by such tests as this: Who could wear a patch, or two extra seams only, over the knee? Most behave as if they believed that their prospects for life would be ruined if they should do it. It would be easier for them to hobble to town with a broken leg than with a broken pantaloon. Often if an accident happens to a gentleman's legs, they can be mended; but if a similar accident happens to the legs of his pantaloons, there is no help for it; for he considers, not what is truly respectable, but what is respected. We know but few men, a great many coats and breeches. Dress a scarecrow in your last shift, you standing shiftless by, who would not soonest salute the scarecrow? . . . It is an interesting question how far men would retain their relative rank if they were divested of their clothes. Could you, in such a case, tell surely of any company of civilized men which belonged to the most respected class?

SINGLE
LINE
TRAFFIC
AHEAD

Ingersoll-

A man who has at length found something to do will not need to get a new suit to do it in; for him the old will do, that has lain dusty in the garret for an indeterminate period. Old shoes will serve a hero longer than they have served his valet—if a hero ever has a valet—bare feet are older than shoes, and he can make them do. Only they who go to soirées and legislative halls must have new coats, coats to change as often as the man changes in them. But if my jacket and trousers, my hat and shoes, are fit to worship God in, they will do; will they not? Who ever saw his old clothes—his old coat, actually worn out, resolved into its primitive elements, so that it was not a deed of charity to bestow it on some poor boy, by him perchance to be bestowed on some poorer still, or shall we say richer, who could do with less? I say, beware of all enterprises that require new clothes, and not rather a new wearer of clothes. If there is not a new man, how can the new clothes be made to fit? If you have any enterprise before you, try it in your old clothes. All men want, not something to *do with,* but something to *do,* or rather something to *be.* Perhaps we should never procure a new suit, however ragged or dirty the old, until we have so conducted, so enterprised or sailed in some way, that we feel like new men in the old, and that to retain it

would be like keeping new wine in old bottles. Our moulting season, like that of the fowls, must be a crisis in our lives. The loon retires to solitary ponds to spend it. Thus also the snake casts its slough, and the caterpillar its wormy coat, by an internal industry and expansion; for clothes are but our outmost cuticle and mortal coil. Otherwise we shall be found sailing under false colors, and be inevitably cashiered at last by our own opinion, as well as that of mankind.

We don garment after garment, as if we grew like exogenous plants by addition without. Our outside and often thin and fanciful clothes are our epidermis, or false skin, which partakes not of our life, and may be stripped off here and there without fatal injury; our thicker garments, constantly worn, are our cellular integument, or cortex; but our shirts are our liber, or true bark, which cannot be removed without girdling and so destroying the man. I believe that all races at some seasons wear something equivalent to the shirt. It is desirable that a man be clad so simply that he can lay his hands on himself in the dark, and that he live in all respects so compactly and preparedly, that, if an enemy take the town, he can, like the old philosopher, walk out the gate empty-handed without anxiety.

Now Mottled Hues Clothe the Earth

As we sweep past the north end of Poplar Hill, with a sandhole in it, its now dryish, pale-brown mottled sward clothing its rounded slope, which was lately saturated with moisture, presents very agreeable hues. In this light, in fair weather, the patches of now dull-greenish mosses contrast just regularly enough with the pale-brown grass. It is like some rich but modest-colored Kidderminster carpet, or rather the skin of a monster python tacked to the hillside and stuffed with earth. These earth colors, methinks, are never so fair as in the spring. Now the green mosses and lichens contrast with the brown grass, but ere long the surface will be uniformly green. I suspect that we are more amused by the effects of color in the skin of the earth now than in summer. . . . Nor are these colors mere thin superficial figures, vehicles for paint, but wonderful living growths—these lichens, to the study of which learned men have devoted their lives—and libraries have been written about them. The earth lies out now like a leopard, drying her lichen and moss spotted skin in the sun, her sleek and variegated hide. I know that the few raw spots will heal over. Brown is the color for me, the color of our coats and our daily lives, the color of the poor man's loaf. The bright tints are pies and cakes, good only for October feasts, which would make us sick if eaten every day.

Old Age

This old man's cheeriness was worth a thousand of the church's sacraments and *memento mori*'s. It was better than a prayerful mood. It proves to me old age as tolerable, as happy, as infancy.

But old age is manlier; it has learned
to live, makes fewer apologies, like infancy.

All Change Is a Miracle to Contemplate

The greater part of what my neighbors call good I believe in my soul to be bad, and if I repent of anything, it is very likely to be my good behavior. What demon possessed me that I behaved so well? You may say the wisest thing you can, old man—you who have lived seventy years, not without honor of a kind—I hear an irresistible voice which invites me away from all that. One generation abandons the enterprises of another like stranded vessels.

I think that we may safely trust a good deal more than we do. We may waive just so much care of ourselves as we honestly bestow elsewhere. Nature is as well adapted to our weakness as to our strength. The incessant anxiety and strain of some is a well-nigh incurable form of disease. We are made to exaggerate the importance of what work we do; and yet how much is not done by us! or, what if we had been taken sick? How vigilant we are! determined not to live by faith if we can avoid it; all the day long on the alert, at night we unwillingly say our prayers and commit ourselves to uncertainties. So thoroughly and sincerely are we compelled to live, reverencing our life, and denying the possibility of change. This is the only way, we say; but there are as many ways as there can be drawn radii from one center. All change is a miracle to contemplate; but it is a miracle which is taking place every instant. Confucius said, "To know that we know what we know, and that we do not know what we do not know, that is true knowledge." When one man has reduced a fact of the imagination to be a fact to his understanding, I foresee that all men will at length establish their lives on that basis.

Let us consider for a moment what most of the trouble and anxiety which I have referred to is about, and how much it is necessary that we be troubled, or at least careful. It would be some advantage to live a primitive and frontier life, though in the midst of an outward civilization, if only to learn what are the gross necessaries of life and what methods have been taken to obtain them; or even to look over the old daybooks of the merchants, to see what it was that men most commonly bought at the stores, what they stored, that is, what are the grossest groceries. For the improvements of ages have had but little influences on the essential laws of man's existence: as our skeletons, probably, are not to be distinguished from those of our ancestors.

Sweet Sylvia!

Even the cat which lies on a rug all day commences to prowl about the fields at night, resumes her ancient forest habits. The most tenderly bred grimalkin steals forth at night—watches some bird on its perch for an hour in the furrow, like a gun at rest. She catches no cold; it is her nature. Caressed by children and cherished with a saucer of milk. Even she can erect her back and expand her tail and spit at her enemies like the wild cat of the woods. Sweet Sylvia!

The Silent Poor

Granted that the *majority* are able at last either to own or hire the modern house with all its improvements. While civilization has been improving our houses, it has not equally improved the men who are to inhabit them. It has created palaces, but it was not so easy to create noblemen and kings. And *if the civilized man's pursuits are no worthier than the savage's, if he is employed the greater part of his life in obtaining gross necessaries and comforts merely, why should he have a better dwelling than the former?*

But how do the poor *minority* fare? Perhaps it will be found that just in proportion as some have been placed in outward circumstances above the savage, others have been degraded below him. The luxury of one class is counterbalanced by the indigence of another. On the one side is the palace, on the other are the almshouse and "silent poor." The myriads who built the pyramids to be the tombs of the Pharaohs were fed on garlic, and it may be were not decently buried themselves. The mason who finishes the cornice of the palace returns at night perchance to a hut not so good as a wigwam. It is a mistake to suppose that, in a country where the usual evidences of civilization exist, the condition of a very large body of the inhabitants may not be as degraded as that of savages. I refer to the degraded poor, not now to the degraded rich. To know this I should not need to look farther than to the shanties which everywhere border our railroads, that last improvement in civilization; where I see in my daily walks human beings living in sties, and all winter with an open door, for the sake of light, without any visible, often imaginable, wood pile, and the forms of both old and young are permanently contracted by the long habit of shrinking from cold and misery, and the development of all their limbs and faculties is checked. It certainly is fair to look at that class by whose labor the works which distinguish this generation are accomplished.

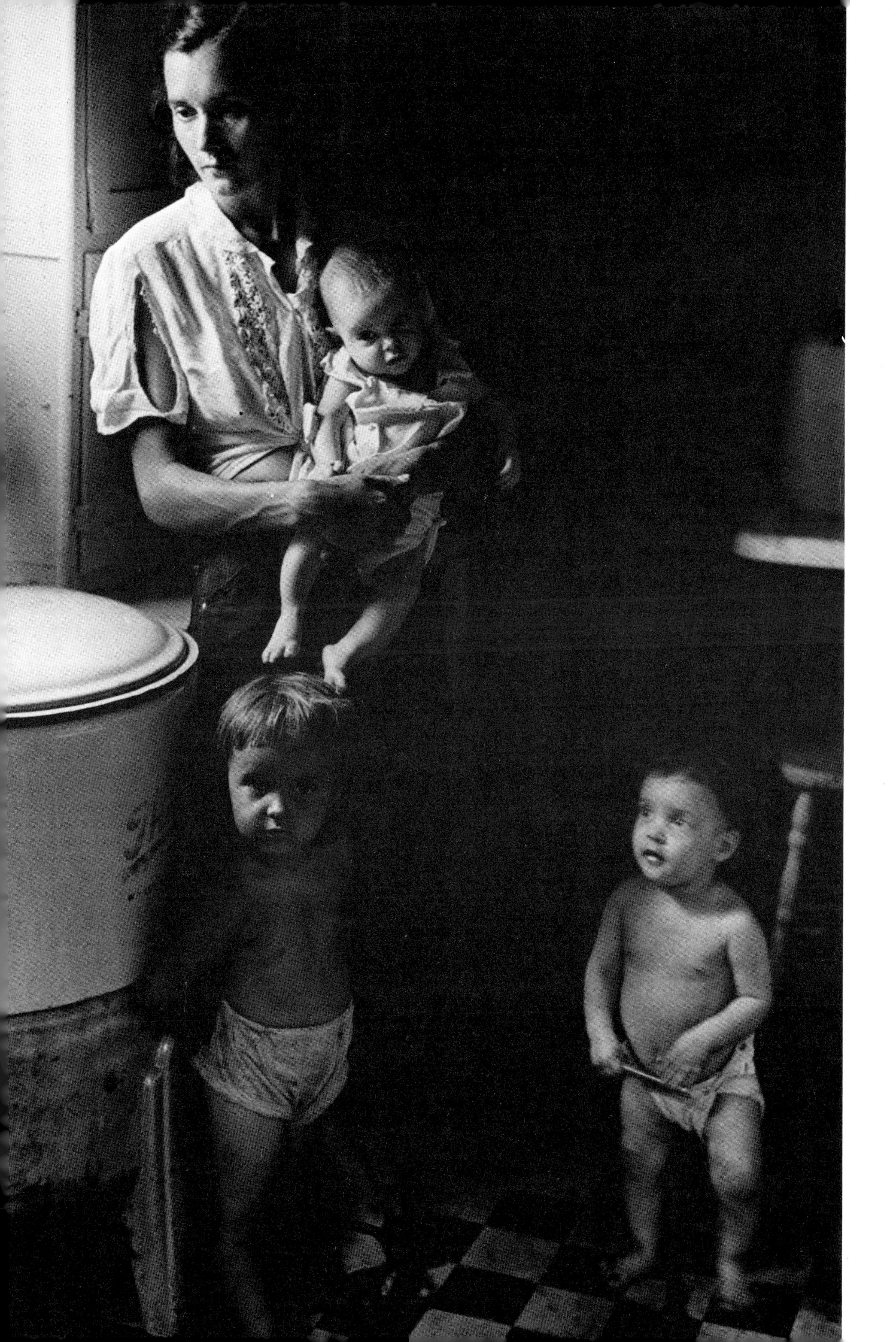

Like Oxen in a Flower Garden

What are the natural features which make a township handsome? A river, with its waterfalls and meadows, a lake, a hill, a cliff or individual rocks, a forest, and ancient trees standing singly. Such things are beautiful; they have a high use which dollars and cents never represent. If the inhabitants of a town were wise, they would seek to preserve these things, though at a considerable expense; for such things educate far more than any hired teachers or preachers, or any at present recognized system of school education.

It would be worth the while if in each town there were a committee appointed to see that the beauty of the town received no detriment. If we have the largest boulder in the county, then it should not belong to an individual, nor be made into doorsteps.

As in many countries precious metals belong to the crown, so here more precious natural objects of rare beauty should belong to the public.

Thus we behave like oxen in a flower garden. The true fruit of Nature can only be plucked with a delicate hand not bribed by any earthly reward, and a fluttering heart. No hired man can help us to gather this crop.

But most men, it seems to me, do not care for Nature and would sell their share in all her beauty, as long as they may live, for a stated sum—many for a glass of rum. Thank God, men cannot as yet fly, and lay waste the sky as well as the earth! We are safe on that side for the present. It is for the very reason that some do not care for those things that we need to continue to protect all from the vandalism of a few.

Civil Disobedience

I heartily accept the motto, "That government is best which governs least"; and I should like to see it acted up to more rapidly and systematically. Carried out, it finally amounts to this, which also I believe—"That government is best which governs not at all"; and when men are prepared for it, that will be the kind of government which they will have. Government is at best but an expedient; but most governments are usually, and all governments are sometimes, inexpedient. The objections which have been brought against a standing army, and they are many and weighty, and deserve to prevail, may also at last be brought against a standing government. The standing army is only an arm of the standing government. The government itself, which is only the mode which the people have chosen to execute their will, is equally liable to be abused and perverted before the people can act through it.

This American government—what is it but a tradition, though a recent one, endeavoring to transmit itself unimpaired to posterity, but each instant losing some of its integrity? It has not the vitality and force of a single living man; for a single man can bend it to his will. It is a sort of wooden gun to the people themselves. But it is not the less necessary for this; for the people must have some complicated machinery or other, and hear its din, to satisfy that idea of government which they

ave. Governments show thus how
uccessfully men can be imposed on, even
npose on themselves, for their own
dvantage. It is excellent, we must all allow.
et this government never of itself
urthered any enterprise, but by the alacrity
ith which it got out of its way. *It* does not
eep the country free. *It* does not settle the
Vest. *It* does not educate. The character
herent in the American people has done
l that has been accomplished; and it
ould have done somewhat more, if the
overnment had not sometimes got in its
ay. For government is an expedient by
hich men would fain succeed in letting
ne another alone; and, as has been said,
hen it is most expedient, the governed are
ost let alone by it. Trade and commerce,
they were not made of india-rubber,
would never manage to bounce over the
obstacles which legislators are continually
putting in their way; and, if one were to
judge these men wholly by the means of
their action and not partly by their
intentions, they would deserve to be
classed and punished with those
mischievous persons who put obstructions
on the railroads.

But, to speak practically and as a citizen,
unlike those who call themselves
no-government men, I ask for, not at once
no government, but *at once* a better
government. Let every man make known
what kind of government would command
his respect, and that will be one step
toward obtaining it.

After all, the practical reason why, when the power is once in the hands of the people, a majority are permitted, and for a long period continue, to rule is not because they are most likely to be in the right, nor because this seems fairest to the minority, but because they are physically the strongest. But a government in which the majority rule in all cases cannot be based on justice, even as far as men understand it. Can there not be a government in which majorities do not virtually decide right and wrong, but conscience?—in which majorities decide only those questions to which the rule of expediency is applicable? Must the citizen ever for a moment, or in the least degree, resign his conscience to the legislator? Why has every man a conscience, then? I think that we should be men first, and subjects afterward. It is not desirable to cultivate a respect for the law, so much as for the right. The only obligation which I have a right to assume is to do at any time what I think right. It is truly enough said that a corporation has no conscience; but a corporation of conscientious men is a corporation *with* a conscience. Law never made men a whit more just; and, by means of their respect for it, even the well-disposed are daily made the agents of injustice. A common and natural result of an undue respect for law is, that you may see a file of soldiers, colonel, captain, corporal, privates, powder-monkeys, and all, marching in admirable order over hill and dale to the wars, against their wills, ay, against their common sense and consciences, which makes it very steep marching indeed, and produces a palpitation of the heart. They have no doubt that it is a damnable business in which they are concerned; they are all peaceably inclined.

I cast my vote, perchance, as I think right; but I am not vitally concerned that that right should prevail. I am willing to leave it to the majority. Its obligation, therefore, never exceeds that of expediency. Even voting *for the right* is *doing* nothing for it. It is only expressing to men feebly your desire that it should prevail. A wise man will not leave the right to the mercy of chance, nor wish it to prevail through the power of the majority. There is but little virtue in the action of masses of men. When the majority shall at length vote for the abolition of slavery, it will be because they are indifferent to slavery, or because there is but little slavery left to be abolished by their vote. *They* will then be the only slaves. Only *his* vote can hasten the abolition of slavery who asserts his own freedom by his vote.

It is not a man's duty, as a matter of course, to devote himself to the eradication of any, even the most enormous, wrong; he may still properly have other concerns to engage him; but it is his duty, at least, to wash his hands of it, and, if he gives it no thought longer, not to give it practically his support. If I devote myself to other pursuits and contemplations, I must first see, at least, that I do not pursue them sitting upon another man's shoulders. I must get off him first, that he may pursue his contemplations too. See what gross inconsistency is tolerated. I have heard some of my townsmen say, "I should like to have them order me out to help put down an insurrection of the slaves, or to march to Mexico—see if I would go"; and yet these very men have each, directly by their allegiance, and so indirectly, at least, by their money, furnished a substitute. The soldier is applauded who refuses to serve in an unjust war by those who do not refuse to sustain the unjust government which makes the war; is applauded by those whose own act and authority he disregards and sets at naught; as if the state were penitent to that degree that it hired one to scourge it while it sinned, but not to that degree that it left off sinning for a moment. Thus, under the name of Order and Civil Government, we are all made at last to pay homage to and support our own meanness. After the first blush of sin comes its indifference; and from immoral it becomes, as it were, *un*moral, and not quite unnecessary to that life which we have made.

Unjust laws exist: shall we be content to obey them, or shall we endeavor to amend them, and obey them until we have succeeded, or shall we transgress them at once? Men generally, under such a government as this, think that they ought to wait until they have persuaded the majority to alter them. They think that, if they should resist, the remedy would be worse than the evil. But it is the fault of the government itself that the remedy *is* worse than the evil. *It* makes it worse. Why is it not more apt to anticipate and provide for reform? Why does it not cherish its wise minority? Why does it cry and resist before it is hurt? Why does it not encourage its citizens to be on the alert to point out its faults, and *do* better than it would have them? Why does it always crucify Christ, and excommunicate Copernicus and Luther, and pronounce Washington and Franklin rebels?

HENRY DAVID THOREAU

was imprisoned for one night in a jail on this site, July, 1846 for refusing to recognize the right of the state to collect taxes from him in support of slavery-an episode made famous in his essay "Civil Disobedience."

Under a government which imprisons any unjustly, the true place for a just man is also a prison. The proper place today, the only place which Massachusetts has provided for her freer and less desponding spirits, is in her prisons, to be put out and locked out of the State by her own act, as they have already put themselves out by their principles. It is there that the fugitive slave, and the Mexican prisoner on parole, and the Indian come to plead the wrongs of his race should find them; on that separate, but more free and honorable, ground, where the State places those who are not *with* her, but *against* her—the only house in a slave State in which a free man can abide with honor. If any think that their influence would be lost there, and their voices no longer afflict the ear of the State, that they would not be as an enemy within its walls, they do not know by how much truth is stronger than error, nor how much more eloquently and effectively he can combat injustice who has experienced a little in his own person. Cast your whole vote, not a strip of paper merely, but your whole influence. A minority is powerless while it conforms to the majority; it is not even a minority then; but it is irresistible when it clogs by its whole weight. If the alternative is to keep all just men in prison, or give up war and slavery, the State will not hesitate which to choose. If a thousand men were not to pay their tax-bills this year, that would not be a violent and bloody measure, as it would be to pay them, and enable the State to commit violence and shed innocent blood. This is, in fact, the definition of a peaceable revolution, if any such is possible. If the tax-gatherer, or any other public officer, asks me, as one has done, "But what shall I do?" my answer is, "If you really wish to do anything, resign your office." When the subject has refused allegiance, and the officer has resigned his office, then the revolution is accomplished. But even suppose blood should flow. Is there not a sort of blood shed when the conscience is wounded? Through this wound a man's real manhood and immortality flow out, and he bleeds to an everlasting death. I see this blood flowing now.

I have contemplated the imprisonment of the offender, rather than the seizure of his goods—though both will serve the same purpose—because they who assert the purest right, and consequently are most dangerous to a corrupt State, commonly have not spent much time in accumulating property. To such the State renders comparatively small service, and a slight tax is wont to appear exorbitant, particularly if they are obliged to earn it by special labor with their hands. If there were one who lived wholly without the use of money, the State itself would hesitate to demand it of him. But the rich man—not to make any invidious comparison—is always sold to the institution which makes him rich. Absolutely speaking, the more money, the less virtue; for money comes between a man and his objects, and obtains them for him; and it was certainly no great virtue to obtain it. It puts to rest many questions which he would otherwise be taxed to answer; while the only new question which it puts is the hard but superfluous one, how to spend it. Thus his moral ground is taken from under his feet.

Thus the State never intentionally confronts a man's sense, intellectual or moral, but only his body, his senses. It is not armed with superior wit or honesty, but with superior physical strength. I was born to be forced. I will breathe after my own fashion. Let us see who is the strongest. What force has a multitude? They only can force me who obey a higher law than I. They force me to become like themselves. I do not hear of *men* being *forced* to live this way or that by masses of men. What sort of life were that to live? When I meet a government which says to me, "Your money or your life," why should I be in haste to give it my money? It may be in a great strait, and not know what to do: I cannot help that. It must help itself; do as I do. It is not worth the while to snivel about it. I am not responsible for the successful working of the machinery of society. I am not the son of the engineer. I perceive that, when an acorn and a chestnut fall side by side, the one does not remain inert to make way for the other, but both obey their own laws, and spring and grow and flourish as best they can, till one, perchance, overshadows and destroys the other. If a plant cannot live according to its nature, it dies; and so a man.

The authority of government, even such as I am willing to submit to—for I will cheerfully obey those who know and can do better than I, and in many things even those who neither know nor can do so well—is still an impure one: to be strictly just, it must have the sanction and consent of the governed. It can have no pure right over my person and property but what I concede to it. The progress from an absolute to a limited monarchy, from a limited monarchy to a democracy, is a progress toward a true respect for the individual. Even the Chinese philosopher was wise enough to regard the individual as the basis of the empire. Is a democracy, such as we know it, the last improvement possible in government? Is it not possible to take a step further towards recognizing and organizing the rights of man? There will never be a really free and enlightened State until the State comes to recognize the individual as a higher and independent power, from which all its own power and authority are derived, and treats him accordingly. I please myself with imagining a State at last which can afford to be just to all men, and to treat the individual with respect as a neighbor; which even would not think it inconsistent with its own repose if a few were to live aloof from it, not meddling with it, nor embraced by it, who fulfilled all the duties of neighbors and fellow men. A State which bore this kind of fruit, and suffered it to drop off as fast as it ripened, would prepare the way for a still more perfect and glorious State, which also I have imagined, but not yet anywhere seen.

The Mists Brood Over Me

I find it good to be out this still, dark, mizzling afternoon; my walk or voyage is more suggestive and profitable than in bright weather. The view is contracted by the misty rain, the water is perfectly smooth, and the stillness is favorable to reflection. I am more open to impressions, more sensitive (not calloused or indurated by sun and wind), as if in a chamber still. My thoughts are concentrated; I am all compact. The solitude is real, too, for the weather keeps other men at home. This mist is like a roof and walls over and around, and I walk with a domestic feeling. The sound of a wagon going over an unseen bridge is louder than ever, and so of other sounds. I am *compelled* to look at near objects. All things have a soothing effect; the very clouds and mists brood over me. My power of observation and contemplation is much increased. My attention does not wander. The world and my life are simplified. What now of Europe and Asia?

Eternal Walden

A lake is the the landscape's most beautiful and expressive feature. It is earth's eye; looking into which the beholder measures the depth of his own nature. The fluviatile trees next the shore are the slender eyelashes which fringe it, and the wooded hills and cliffs around are its overhanging brows.

Standing on the smooth sandy beach at the east end of the pond, in a calm September afternoon, when a slight haze makes the opposite shore line indistinct, I have seen whence came the expression, "the glassy surface of a lake." When you invert your head, it looks like a thread of finest gossamer stretched across the valley, and gleaming against the distant pine woods, separating one stratum of the atmosphere from another. You would think that you could walk dry under it to the opposite hills, and that the swallows which skim over might perch on it. Indeed, they sometimes dive below the line, as it were by mistake, and are undeceived.

As you look over the pond westward you are obliged to employ both your hands to defend your eyes against the reflected as well as the true sun, for they are equally bright; and if, between the two, you survey its surface critically, it is literally as smooth as glass, except where the skater insects, at equal intervals scattered over its whole extent, by their motions in the sun produce the finest imaginable sparkle on it, or, perchance, a duck plumes itself, or, as I have said, a swallow skims so low as to touch it. It may be that in the distance a fish describes an arc of three or four feet in the air, and there is one bright flash where it emerges, and another where it strikes the water; sometimes the whole silvery arc is revealed; or here and there, perhaps, is a thistledown floating on its surface, which the fishes dart at and so dimple it again. It is like molten glass cooled but not congealed, and the few motes in it are pure and beautiful like the imperfections in glass. You may often detect a yet smoother and darker water, separated from the rest as if by an invisible cobweb, boon of the water nymphs, resting on it. . . . How peaceful the phenomena of the lake! Again the works of man shine as in the spring. Ay, every leaf and twig and stone and cobweb sparkles now at mid-afternoon as when covered with dew in a spring morning. Every motion of an oar or an insect produces a flash of light; and if an oar falls, how sweet the echo!

In such a day, in September or October, Walden is a perfect forest mirror, set round with stones as precious to my eye as if fewer or rarer. Nothing so fair, so pure, and at the same time so large, as a lake, perchance, lies on the surface of the earth. Sky water. It needs no fence. Nations come and go without defiling it. It is a mirror which no stone can crack, whose quicksilver will never wear off, whose gilding Nature continually repairs; no storms, no dust, can dim its surface ever fresh; a mirror in which all impurity presented to it sinks, swept and dusted by the sun's hazy brush—this the light dustcloth—which retains no breath that is breathed on it, but sends its own to float as clouds high above its surface, and be reflected in its bosom still.

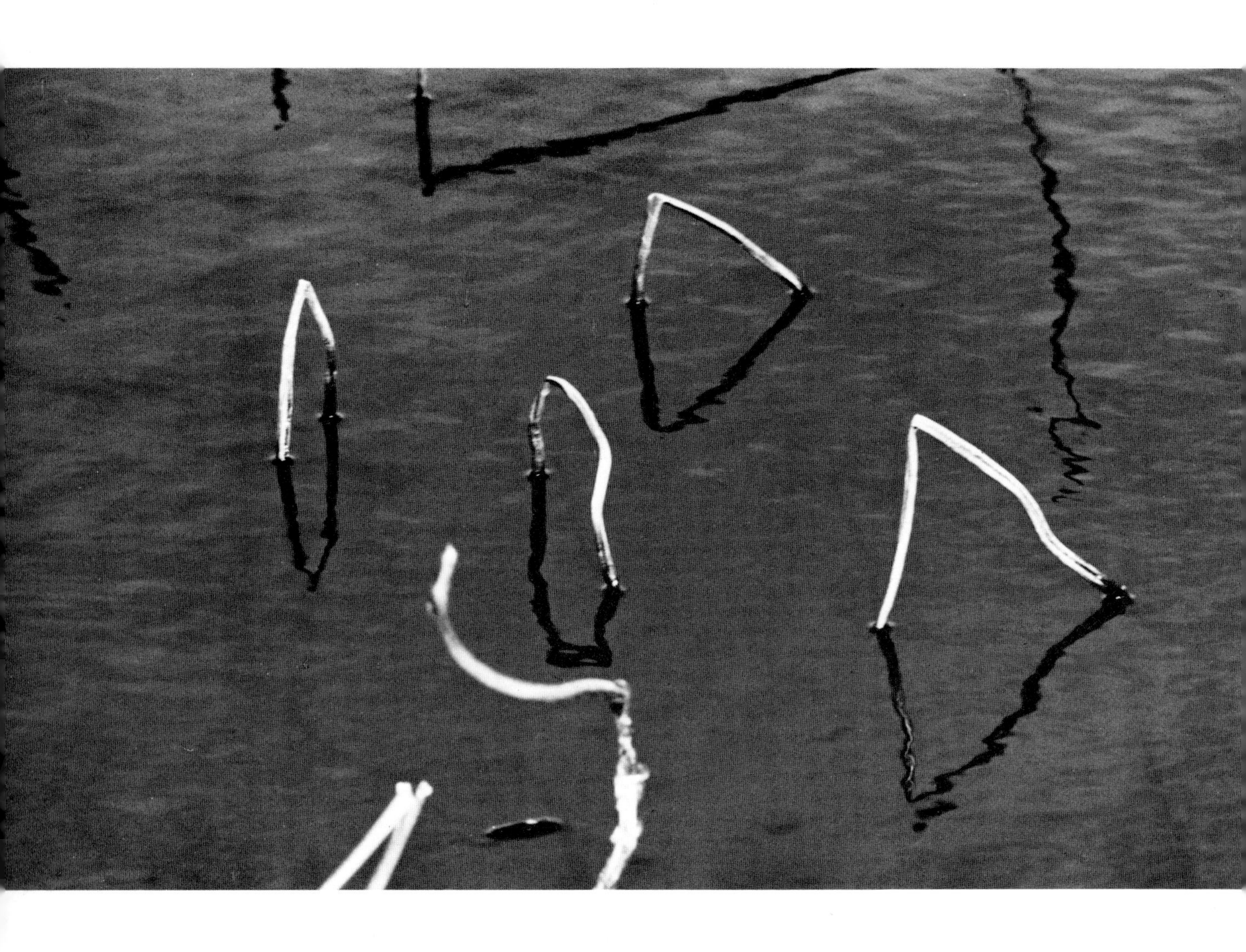

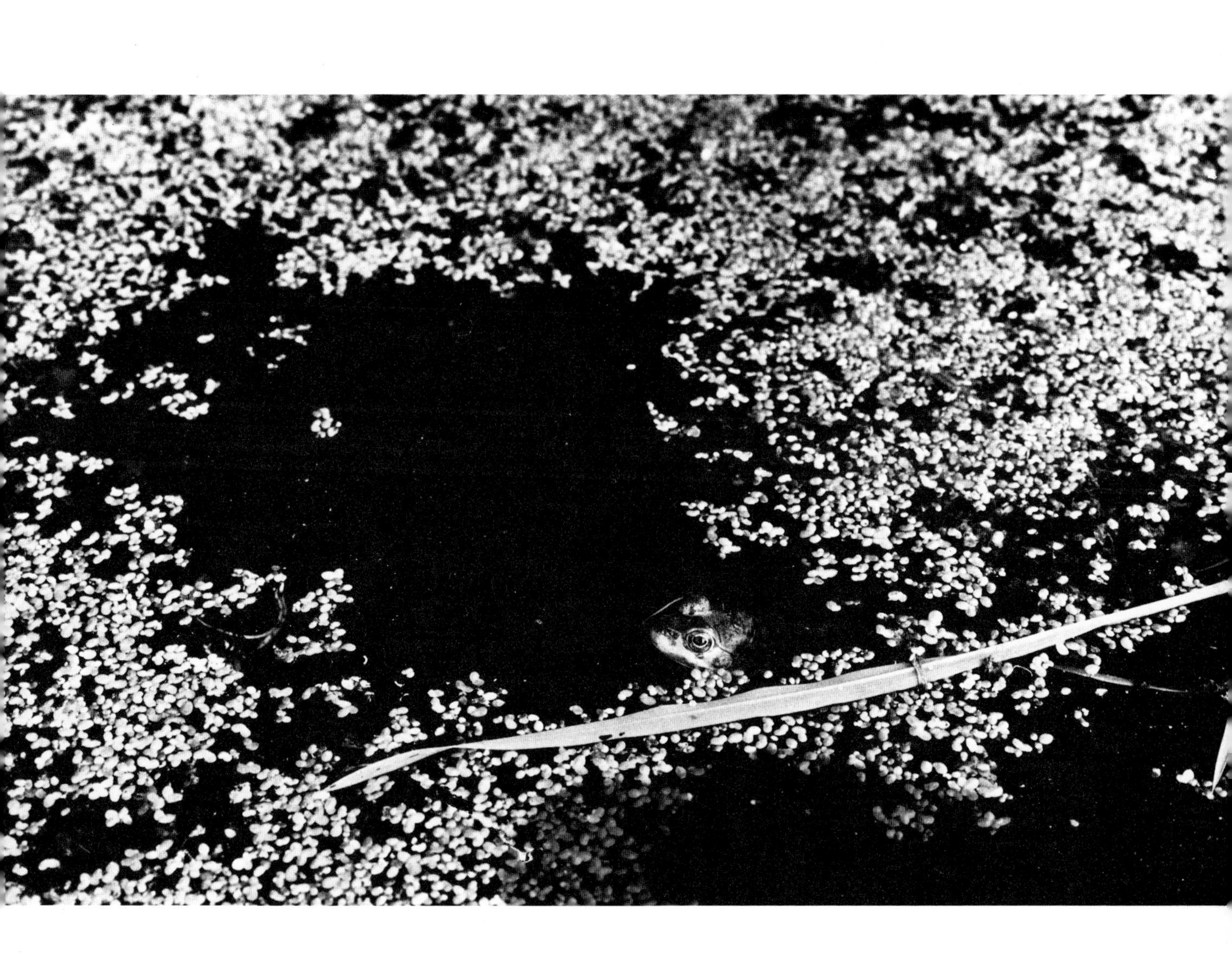

A field of water betrays the spirit that is in the air. It is continually receiving new life and motion from above. It is intermediate in its nature between land and sky. On land only the grass and trees wave, but the water itself is rippled by the wind. I see where the breeze dashes across it by the streaks or flakes of light. It is remarkable that we can look down on its surface. We shall, perhaps, look down thus on the surface of air at length, and mark where a still subtler spirit sweeps over it.

The scenery of Walden is on a humble scale, and, though very beautiful, does not approach to grandeur, nor can it much concern one who has not long frequented it or lived by its shore; yet this pond is so remarkable for its depth and purity as to merit a particular description. It is a clear and deep green well, half a mile long and a mile and three quarters in circumference, and contains about sixty-one and a half acres; a perennial spring in the midst of pine and oak woods, without any visible inlet or outlet except by the clouds and evaporation. The surrounding hills rise abruptly from the water to the height of forty to eighty feet, though on the southeast and east they attain to about one hundred and one hundred and fifty feet respectively, within a quarter and a third of a mile. They are exclusively woodland. . . . Walden is blue at one time and green at another, even from the same point of view. Lying between the earth and the heavens, it partakes of the color of both. Viewed from a hilltop it reflects the color of the sky; but near at hand it is of a yellowish tint next the shore where you can see the sand, then a light green, which gradually deepens to a uniform dark green in the body of the pond. In some lights, viewed even from a hilltop, it is of a vivid green next the shore. Some have referred this to the reflection of the verdure; but it is equally green there against the railroad sand-bank, and in the spring, before the leaves are expanded, and it may be simply the result of the prevailing blue mixed with the yellow of the sand. Such is the color of its iris. This is that portion, also, where in the spring, the ice being warmed by the heat of the sun reflected from the bottom, and also transmitted through the earth, melts first and forms a narrow canal about the still frozen middle.

To See the Spring Come In

One attraction in coming to the woods to live was that I should have leisure and opportunity to see the Spring come in. The ice in the pond at length begins to be honeycombed, and I can set my heel in it as I walk. Fogs and rains and warmer suns are gradually melting the snow; the days have grown sensibly longer; and I see how I shall get through the winter without adding to my woodpile, for large fires are no longer necessary. I am on the alert for the first signs of spring, to hear the chance note of some arriving bird, or the striped squirrel's chirp, for his stores must be now nearly exhausted, or see the woodchuck venture out of his winter quarters. On the 13th of March, after I had heard the bluebird, song-sparrow, and red-wing, the ice was still nearly a foot thick. As the weather grew warmer it was not sensibly worn away by the water, nor broken up and floated off as in rivers, but, though it was completely melted for half a rod in width about the shore, the middle was merely honeycombed and saturated with water, so that you could put your foot through it when six inches thick; but by the next day evening, perhaps, after a warm rain followed by fog, it would have wholly disappeared, all gone off with the fog, spirited away.

Every incident connected with the breaking up of the rivers and ponds and the settling of the weather is particularly interesting to us who live in a climate of so great extremes. When the warmer days come, they who dwell near the river hear the ice crack at night with a startling whoop as loud as artillery, as if its icy fetters were rent from end to end, and within a few days see it rapidly going out. So the alligator comes out of the mud with quakings of the earth.

I Left the Woods

I left the woods for as good a reason as I went there. Perhaps it seemed to me that I had several more lives to live, and could not spare any more time for that one. It is remarkable how easily and insensibly we fall into a particular route, and make a beaten track for ourselves. I had not lived there a week before my feet wore a path from my door to the pond-side; and though it is five or six years since I trod it, it is still quite distinct. It is true, I fear that others may have fallen into it, and so helped to keep it open. The surface of the earth is soft and impressible by the feet of men; and so with the paths which the mind travels. How worn and dusty, then, must be the highways of the world, how deep the ruts of tradition and conformity! I did not wish to take a cabin passage, but rather to go before the mast and on the deck of the world, for there I could best see the moonlight amid the mountains. I do not wish to go below now.

I learned this, at least, by my experiment; that if one advances confidently in the direction of his dreams, and endeavors to live the life which he has imagined, he will meet with a success unexpected in common hours. He will put some things behind, will pass an invisible boundary; new, universal, and more liberal laws will begin to establish themselves around and within him; or the old laws be expanded, and interpreted in his favor in a more liberal sense, and he will live with the license of a higher order of beings. In proportion as he simplifies his life, the laws of the universe will appear less complex, and solitude will not be solitude, nor poverty poverty, nor weakness weakness. If you have built castles in the air, your work need not be lost; that is where they should be. Now put the foundations under them.

A Different Drummer

Why should we be in such desperate haste to succeed and in such desperate enterprises? If a man does not keep pace with his companions, perhaps it is because he hears a different drummer. Let him step to the music which he hears, however measured or far away. It is not important that he should mature as soon as an apple tree or an oak. Shall he turn his spring into summer? If the condition of things which we were made for is not yet, what were any reality which we can substitute? We will not be shipwrecked on a vain reality. Shall we with pains erect a heaven of blue glass over ourselves, though when it is done we shall be sure to gaze still at the true ethereal heaven far above, as if the former were not?

However mean your life is, meet it and live it; do not shun it and call it hard names. It is not so bad as you are. It looks poorest when you are richest. The fault-finder will find faults even in paradise. Love your life, poor as it is. You may perhaps have some pleasant, thrilling, glorious hours, even in a poorhouse. The setting sun is reflected from the windows of the almshouse as brightly as from the rich man's abode; the snow melts before its door as early in the spring. I do not see but a quiet mind may live as contentedly there, and have as cheering thoughts, as in a palace. The town's poor seem to me often to live the most independent lives of any. Maybe they are simply great enough to receive without misgiving. Most think that they are above being supported by the town; but it oftener happens that they are not above supporting themselves by dishonest means, which should be more disreputable. Cultivate poverty like a garden herb, like sage. Do not trouble yourself much to get new things, whether clothes or friends. Turn the old; return to them. Things do not change; we change. Sell your clothes and keep your thoughts. God will see that you do not want society. If I were confined to a corner of a garret all my days, like a spider, the world would be just as large to me while I had my thoughts about me. The philosopher said: "From an army of three divisions one can take away its general, and put it in disorder; from the man the most abject and vulgar one cannot take away his thought." Do not seek so anxiously to be developed, to subject yourself to many influences to be played on; it is all dissipation. Humility like darkness reveals the heavenly lights. The shadows of poverty and meanness gather around us, "and lo! creation widens to our view." We are often reminded that if there were bestowed on us the wealth of Croesus, our aims must still be the same, and our means essentially the same. Moreover, if you are restricted in your range by poverty, if you cannot buy books and newspapers, for instance, you are but confined to the most significant and vital experiences; you are compelled to deal with the material which yields the most sugar and the most starch. It is life near the bone where it is sweetest. You are defended from being a trifler. No man loses ever on a lower level by magnanimity on a higher. Superfluous wealth can buy superfluities only. Money is not required to buy one necessary of the soul.

THOREAU'S VISION OF THE NATURAL WORLD

by Loren Eiseley

I THE CONCORD LYNX

Somewhere, in the coverts about Concord, a lynx was killed well over a century ago and examined by Henry David Thoreau; measured, in fact, and meditated upon from nose to tail. Others called it a Canadian lynx, far strayed from the northern wilds. No, insisted Thoreau positively, it is indigenous, indigenous but rare. It is a night haunter; it is a Concord lynx. On this he was adamant. Just this spring over in Vermont, an intelligent college girl told me that, walking in the woods, her Labrador retriever had startled and been attacked by a Canadian lynx which she had been fully competent to recognize. I was too shy, however, to raise the question of whether the creature might have been, as Thoreau defiantly asserted, a genuine New England lynx, persisting but rare since colonial times.

Thoreau himself was a genuine Concord lynx. Of that there can be no doubt. We know the place of his birth, his rarity, something of his habits, his night travels, that he had, on occasion, a snarl transferred to paper, and that he frequented swamps, abandoned cellar holes, and woodlots. His temperament has been a subject of much uncertainty, as much, in truth, as the actual shape of those human figures which he was wont to examine looming in fogs or midsummer hazes. Thoreau sometimes had difficulty in seeing men or, by contrast, sometimes saw them too well. Others had difficulty in adjusting their vision to the Concord lynx himself, with the result that a varied and contentious literature has come down to us. Even the manner of his death is uncertain, for though the cause is known, some have maintained that he benefited a weak constitution by a rugged outdoor life. Others contend that he almost deliberately stoked the fires of consumption by prolonged exposure in inclement weather.

As is the case with most wild animals at the periphery of the human vision, Thoreau's precise temperament is equally a matter of conjecture even though he left several books and a seemingly ingenuous journal which one eminent critic, at least, regards as a cunningly contrived mythology. He has been termed a stoic, a contentious moralizer, a parasite, an arsonist, a misanthrope, a supreme egotist, a father-hater who projected his animus on the state, a banal writer who somehow managed to produce a classic work of literature. He has also been described as a philosophical anarchist and small-town failure, as well as an intellectual aristocrat. Some would classify him simply as a nature writer, others as a failed scientist who did not comprehend scientific method. Others speak of his worldwide influence upon the social movements of the twentieth century, of his exquisite insight and style, of his relentless searching for something never found, a mystic in the best sense of the term. He has also been labeled a prig by a notable man of English letters. There remains from those young people who knew him the utterly distinct view that he was a friendly, congenial, and kindly man. At the time of his funeral, and long before fame attended his memory, the schools of Concord were dismissed in his honor.

The above essay was delivered at the Annual Meeting of the Thoreau Society on July 14, 1973, at Concord, Massachusetts.

In short, the Concord lynx did not go unwept to his grave. Much of the later controversy that has created a Browningesque *Ring and the Book* atmosphere about his intentions and character are the product of a sophisticated literary world he abhorred in life. Something malevolent frequently creeps into this atmosphere even though it is an inevitable accompaniment of the transmission of great books through the ages. Basically the sensitive writer should stay away from his own kind. Jealousies, tensions, feuds, unnecessary discourtesies that are hard to bear in print are frequently augmented by close contact, even if friendships begin well. The writer's life is a lonely one and doubtless should remain so, but a prurient curiosity allows no great artist to rest easy in his grave. Critical essays upon Thoreau now number hundreds of items, very little of which, I suspect, would move the Concord lynx to do more than retire further into whatever thickets might remain to him. Neither science nor literature were his total concern. He was, as I have written elsewhere, a fox at the wood's edge, regarding human preoccupations with doubt. Indeed he had rejected an early invitation to join the American Association for the Advancement of Science. The man had never entertained illusions about the course of technological progress and, like an Indian, the only message he had gotten from the telegraph was the song of the wind through its wires.

As a naturalist he possessed the kind of memory which fixes certain scenes in the mind forever—a feeling for the vastness and mystery contained in nature, a powerful aesthetic response when, in his own words, "a thousand bare twigs gleam like cobwebs in the sun." He had been imprinted, as it were, by his home landscape at an early age. Similarly, whatever I may venture upon the meaning of Thoreau must come basically from memory alone, with perhaps some examination of the tone of his first journal as contrasted with his last. My present thoughts convey only the residue of what, in the course of time, I have come to feel about his intellectual achievement—the solitary memory that Thoreau himself might claim of a journey across austere uplands.

In addition, my observations come mostly from the realm of science, whereas the preponderance of what had been written about Thoreau has come from the region he appeared to inhabit: namely, literature. His scientific interests have frequently been denigrated, and he himself is known more than once to have deplored the "inhumanity of science." Surely then, one cannot, as a representative of this alien discipline, be accused of either undue tolerance or weak sympathy for a transcendental idealism that has largely fallen out of fashion. Yet it is of an aspect of this philosophy, more particularly as it is found modified in Thoreau, that I would speak. For Thoreau, like Emerson, is an anticipator, a forerunner of the process philosophers who have so largely dominated the twentieth century. He stands at the border between existent and potential nature.

II THE PASSPORT

Behind all religions lurks the concept of nature. It persists equally in the burial cults of Neanderthal man, in Cro-Magnon hunting art, in the questions of Job and in the answering voice from the whirlwind. In the end it is the name of man's attempt to define and delimit his world, whether seen or unseen. He knows intuitively that nature is a reality which existed before him and will survive his individual death. He may include in his definition that which is, or that which may be. Nature remains an otherness which incorporates man, but which man instinctively feels contains secrets denied to him.

A professional atheist must still account for the fleeting particles that appear and vanish in the perfected cyclotrons of modern physics. We may see behind nature a divinity which rules it, or we may regard nature itself as a somewhat nebulous and ill-defined deity. Man knows he springs from nature and not nature from him. This is very old and primitive knowledge. Man, as the "thinking reed," the memory beast, and the anticipator of things to come, has devised hundreds of cosmogonies and interpretations of nature. More lately, with the dawn of the scientific method, he has sought to probe nature's secrets by experiment rather than unbounded speculation.

Still, of all words coming easily to the tongue, none is more mysterious, none more elusive. Behind nature is hidden the chaos as well as the regularities of the world. And behind all that is evident to our senses is veiled the insubstantial deity that only man of all earth's creatures, has had the power to either perceive or project into nature.

As scientific agnostics we may draw an imaginary line beyond which we deny ourselves the right to pass. We may adhere to the tangible, but we will still be forced to speak of the "unknowable" or of "final causes" even if we proclaim such phrases barren and of no concern to science. In our minds we will acknowledge a line we have drawn, a definition to which we have arbitrarily restricted ourselves, a human limit that may or may not coincide with reality. It will still be nature that concerns us as it concerned the Neanderthal. We cannot exorcise the word, refine it semantically though we may. Nature is the receptacle that contains man and into which he finally sinks to rest. It implies all, absolutely all, that man knows or can know. The word ramifies and runs through the centuries assuming different connotations.

Sometimes it appears as ghostly as the unnamed shadow behind it; sometimes it appears harsh, prescriptive, and solid. Again matter becomes interchangeable with energy; fact becomes shadow, law becomes probability. Nature is a word that must have arisen with man. It is part of his otherness, his humanity. Other beasts live within nature. Only man has ceaselessly turned the abstraction round and round upon his tongue and found fault with every definition, found himself looking ceaselessly outside of nature toward something invisible to any eye but his own and indeed not surely to be glimpsed by him.

To propound that Henry David Thoreau is a process philosopher, it is necessary first to understand something of the concepts entertained by early nineteenth-century science and philosophy, and also to consider something of the way in which these intellectual currents were changing. New England's ties to English thought preponderated, although, as is well known, some of the ideas had their roots on the continent. An exhaustive analysis is unnecessary to our present purpose. Thoreau was a child of his time but he also reached beyond it.

In early nineteenth-century British science there was a marked obsession with Baconian induction. The more conservative minded, who dreaded the revelations of the new geology, sought, in their emphatic demand for facts, to drive wide ranging and useful hypotheses out of currency. The thought of Bacon, actually one of the innovators of scientific method, was being perverted into a convenient barrier against the advance of irreligious science. Robert Chambers, an early evolutionist, had felt the weight of this criticism, and Darwin, later on, experienced it beyond the midcentury. In inexperienced hands it led to much aimless fact gathering under the guise of proper inductive procedures for true scientists. Some, though not all, of Thoreau's compendiums and detailed observations suggest this view of science, just as do his occasional scornful remarks about museum taxonomy.
In a typical Thoreauvian paradox he could neither leave his bundles of accumulated fact alone, nor resist muttering "it is ebb tide with the scientific reports." Only toward the close of his journals does he seem to be inclining toward a more perceptive scientific use of his materials under the influence of later reading. It is necessary to remember that most of Thoreau's intellectual contacts were with literary men, though Emerson was a wide and eclectic reader who saw clearly that the new uniformitarian geology had transformed our conceptions of the world's antiquity.

The one striking exception to Thoreau's lack of direct contact with the scientific world was his meeting with Louis Agassiz after the European glaciologist, taxonomist, and teacher had joined the staff at Harvard in the 1840s. Brilliant and distinguished naturalist though he was, Louis Agassiz was probably not the best influence upon Thoreau. He traced the structural relations of living things, he introduced America to comparative taxonomy, he taught Thoreau to observe such oddities as frozen and revived caterpillars. His eye, if briefly, was added to Thoreau's eye, not always to the latter's detriment. Typically, Agassiz warned against hasty generalizations while pursuing relentlessly his own interpretation of nature.

The European poet of the Ice Age was, in a very crucial sense, at the same time an anachronism. He did not believe in evolution; he did not grasp the significance of natural selection. "Geology," he wrote in 1857, "only shows that at different periods there have existed different species; but no transition from those of a preceding into those of a following epoch has ever been noticed anywhere. . . ." He saw a beneficent intelligence behind nature; he was a Platonist at heart, dealing with the classification of the eternal forms, seeing in the vestigial organs noted by the evolutionist only the direct evidence of divine plan carried through for symmetry's sake even when the organ was functionless.

It is this preternatural intelligence which Thoreau is led to see in the protective arrangement of moth cocoons in winter. "What kind of understanding," he writes, "was there between the mind . . . and that of the worm that fastened a few of these leaves to its cocoon in order to disguise it?" Plainly he is following in the footsteps of the great biologist, who, as many other scholars were first to do, recognized a spiritual succession of forms in the strata, but not the genuine organic transformations that had produced the living world. It may be noted in passing that this Platonic compromise with reality was one easily acceptable to most transcendentalists. They were part of a far-removed Romantic movement which was to find the mechanistic aspects of nineteenth-century science increasingly intolerable. One need not align oneself totally with every aspect of the Darwinian universe, however, to see that Agassiz's particular teleological interpretation of nature could not be long sustained. Whatever might lie behind the incredible profusion of living forms would not so easily yield its secrets to man.

The mystery in nature Thoreau began to sense early. A granitic realism forced from him the recognition that the natural world is indifferent to human morality, just as the young Darwin had similarly brooded over the biological imperfections and savagery of the organic realm. "How can [man]" protested Thoreau, "perform that long journey who has not conceived whither he is bound, . . . who has no passport to the end?" This is a far cry from the expressions of some of Thoreau's contemporary transcendentalists who frequently confused nature with a hypostatized divine Reason which man could activate within himself. By contrast, Thoreau remarks wearily, "Is not disease the rule of existence?" He had seen the riddled leaf and the worm-infested bud.

If one meditates upon the picture of nature presented by both the transcendental thinkers such as Emerson and the evolutionary doctrine drawn from Darwin, one is struck by the contrast between what appears to be a real and an ideal nature. The transcendentalist lived in two worlds at once; in one of which he was free to transform himself, he could escape the ugly determinism of the real. In Emerson's words "two states of thought diverge every moment in wild contrast."

The same idea is echoed in the first volume of his journals when the young Thoreau ventures, "On one side of man is the actual and on the other the ideal." These peculiar worlds are simultaneously existent. Life is bifurcated between the observational world and another more ideal but realizable set of "instructions" implanted in our minds, again a kind of Platonic blueprint. We must be taught through the proper understanding of the powers within us. The transcendentalist possessed the strong optimism of the early Republic, the belief in an earthly Eden to be created.

If we examine the Darwinian world of change we recognize that the nature of the evolutionary process is such as to deny any relationships except those that can be established on purely phyletic grounds of uninterrupted descent. The Platonic abstract blueprint of successive types has been dismissed as a hopeful fiction. Vestigial organs are really what their name implies—remnants lingering from a former state of existence. The tapeworm, the sleeping sickness trypanosome, are as much a product of natural selection as man himself. All currently existing animals and plants have ancestral roots extending back into Archeozoic time. Every species is, in some degree, imperfect and scheduled to vanish by reason of the very processes which brought it into being. Even in this world of endless struggle, however, Darwin is forced to introduce a forlorn note of optimism which appears in the final pages of *The Origin of Species*. It is his own version of the ideal. Out of the war of nature, of strife unending, he declares, all things will progress toward perfection.

The remark rings somewhat hollowly upon the ear. Darwin's posited ideal world, such as it is, offers no immediate hope that man can embrace. Indeed, it is proffered on the same page where Darwin indicates that of the species now living very few will survive into the remote future. Teleological direction has been read out of the universe. It would reemerge later on in the twentieth century in more sophisticated guises that would have entranced Thoreau, but for the moment the "Great Companion" was dead. The Darwinian circle had introduced process into nature, but they had never paused to examine nature itself. In the words of Alfred North Whitehead, "Science is concerned not with the causes but the coherence of nature." Something, in other words, held the thing called nature together, gave it duration in the midst of change and a queer kind of inhuman rationality.

It may be true enough that Thoreau in his last years never resolved his philosophical difficulties. (Indeed, what man has?) It may also be assumed that the confident and brilliant perceptions of the young writer began to give way in his middle years to a more patient search for truth. The scientist in him was taking the place of the artist. To some of the literary persuasion this may seem a great loss. Considering, however, the toils from which he freed himself, the hope that he renewed, his solitary achievement is remarkable.

One may observe that there are two reigning models involving human behavior today: a conservative and a progressive version. The first may be stated as regarding man in the mass as closely reflecting his primate origins. He is the "ape and tiger" of Huxley's writing. His origins are sufficiently bestial that they place limits upon his ethical possibilities. Latent aggression makes him an uncertain and dangerous creature.

Unconsciously, perhaps, the first evolutionists sought to link man more closely to the animal world from which he had arisen. Paradoxically this conception would literally freeze man upon his evolutionary pathway as thoroughly as though a similar argument had been projected upon him when he was a Cretaceous tree shrew. Certainly one may grant our imperfect nature. Man is in process, as is the whole of life. He may survive or he may not, but so long as he survives he will be part of the changing, onrushing future. He, too, will be subject to alteration. In fact, he may now be approaching the point of consciously inducing his own modification.

How did Thoreau, who matured under the influence of the transcendentalists and the design arguments of Louis Agassiz, react to this shifting, oncoming world of contingency and change? It is evident he was familiar with Charles Lyell's writings, that he knew about the development (i.e., evolution) theories of Robert Chambers. The final volume of his journals even suggests that he may have meditated upon Darwin's views before his death in 1862.

Now, in the final years, he seems to gather himself for one last effort. "The development theory implies a greater vital force in nature," he writes, "because it is more flexible and accommodating and equivalent to a sort of constant new creation."

He recognizes the enormous waste in nature, but tries carefully to understand its significance just as he grasps the struggle for existence. His eyes are open still to his tenderly cherished facts of snow and leaves and seasons. He counts tree rings and tries to understand forest succession. The world is perhaps vaster than he imagined, but even from the first, nature was seen as lawless on occasion and capable of cherishing unimaginable potentials. That was where he chose to stand, at the very edge of the future, "to anticipate," as he says in *Walden,* "nature herself."

This is not the conservative paradigm of the neo-Darwinian circle. Instead it clearly forecasts the thought of twentieth-century Alfred North Whitehead. Thoreau strove with an unequaled intensity to observe nature in all its forms, whether in the raw shapes of mountains or the travelings of seeds and deer mice. His consciousness expanded like a sunflower. The more objects he beheld the more immortal he became. "My senses," he wrote, "get no rest." It was as though he had foreseen Whitehead's dictum that "passage is a quality not only of nature, which is the thing known, but also of sense awareness which is the procedure of knowing." Thoreau had constituted himself the Knower. "All change," he wrote, "is a miracle to contemplate, but it is a miracle that is taking place every instant." He saw man thrust up through the crust of nature "like a wedge and not till the wound heals . . . do we begin to discover where we are." He viewed us all as mere potential; shadowy, formless perhaps, but as though about to be formed. He had listened alone to the "unspeakable rain," he had sought in his own way to lead others to a supernatural life in nature. He had succeeded. He had provided the passport for others that at first he thought did not exist; a passport, he finally noted, "earned from the elements."

III THE EYE

Following the involved saunterings of the journals is to observe a man sorting, selecting, questioning less nature than his own way into nature, to find, as Thoreau expressed it, "a patent for himself." Thoreau is never wholly a man of the transcendental camp. He is, in a sense, a double agent. He is drawn both to the spiritual life and to that of the savage. "Are we not all wreckers," he asks, "and do we not contract the habits of wreckers?" The term *wreckers,* of course, he uses in the old evil sense of the shore scavengers who with false lights beckoned ships to their doom. And again he queries, "Is our life innocent enough?" It would appear he thinks otherwise for he writes, "I have a murderer's experience . . ." and he adds, a trifle scornfully, "there is no record of a great success in history."

Thoreau once said disconsolately that he awaited a Visitor who never came, one whom he referred to as the "Great Looker." Some have thought that pique or disappointment shows in these words and affects his subsequent work. I do not choose to follow this line of reasoning for, on another page of *Walden,* he actually recollects receiving his guest as the "old settler and original proprietor who is reported to have dug Walden pond . . . and fringed it with pine woods." As a somewhat heretical priest once observed, "God asks nothing of the highest soul but attention."

Supplementing that remark Thoreau had asserted, "There has been nothing but the sun and the eye since the beginning." That eye, in the instance of Thoreau, had missed nothing. Even in the depths of winter when nature's inscriptions lay all about him in the snow, he had not faltered to recognize among them the cruel marks of a farmer's whip, steadily, even monotonously, lashing his oxen down the drift-covered road. The sight wounded him. Nature, he knew, was not bound to be kind to man. In fact, there was a kind of doubleness in nature as in the writer. The inner eye was removed, its qualities were more than man, as natural man, could long sustain. The Visitor had come in human guise and looked out upon the world a few brief summers. It is remembered that when at last an acquaintance came to ask of Thoreau on his deathbed if he had made his peace with God, the Visitor in him responded simply, "We have never quarreled."

Thoreau had appropriated the snow as "the great revealer." On it were inscribed all the hieroglyphs that the softer seasons concealed. Last winter, trudging in the woods, I came to a spot where freezing, melting, and refreezing had lifted old footprints into little pinnacles of trapped oak leaves as though a shrub oak had walked upon some errand. Thoreau had recorded the phenomenon over a century ago. There was something uncanny about it, I thought, standing attentively in the snow. A visitor, perhaps the Visitor, had once more passed.

In the very first volume of his journals Thoreau had written, "There is always the possibility, the possibility, I say, of being all, or remaining a particle in the universe." He had, in the end, learned that nature was not an enlarged version of the human ego, that it was not, to use Emerson's phrase, "the immense shadow of man." Toward the close of his life he had turned from literature to the growing, formidable world of the new science—the science that later on in the twentieth century was destined to reduce everything to infinitesimal particles and finally these to a universal vortex of wild energies.

But the eye persisted, the unexplainable eye that gave even Darwin a cold shudder. All it experienced were the secondary qualities, the illusions that physics had rejected, but the eye remained, just as Thoreau had asserted—the sun and the eye from the beginning. Thoreau was gone, but the eye was multitudinous, ineradicable.

I advanced upon the fallen oak leaves. We were all the eye of the Visitor—the eye whose reason no physics could explain. Generation after generation the eye was among us. We were particles but we were also the recording eye that saw the sunlight —that which physics had reduced to cold waves in a cold void. Thoreau's life had been dedicated to the unexplainable eye.

I had been trained since youth against the illusions, the deceptions of that eye, against sunset as reality, against my own features as anything but a momentary midge-swarm of particles. Even this momentary phantasm I saw by the mind's eye alone. I no longer resisted as I walked. I went slowly, making sure that the eye momentarily residing in me saw and recorded what was intended when Thoreau spoke of the quality of the eye as belonging more to God than man.

But there was a message Thoreau intended to transmit. "I suspect," he had informed his readers, "that if you should go to the end of the world, you would find somebody there going further." It is plain that he wanted a message carried that distance but what was it? We are never entirely certain. He delighted in gnomic utterances such as that in which he pursued the summer on snowshoes.

"I do not think much of the actual," he had added. Is this then the only message of the great Walden traveler in the winter days when the years "came fast as snowflakes"? Perhaps it is so intended, but the words remain cryptic. Thoreau, as is evidenced by his final journals, had labored to lay the foundations of an as yet unnamed new science—ecology. In many ways he had outlived his century. He was always concerned with the actual, but it was the unrolling reality of the process philosopher, "the universe," as he says, "that will not wait to be explained."

For this reason he tended to see men at a distance. For the same reason he saw himself as a first settler in nature, his house the oldest in the settlement. Thoreau reflected in his mind the dreamers of the westward crossing; in this he is totally American.

Yet Thoreau preferred to the end his own white winter spaces. He lingers, curvetting gracefully, like the fox he saw on the river or the falcon in the morning air. He identifies, he enters them, he widens the circumference of life to its utmost bounds. "One world at a time," he jokes playfully on his deathbed, but it is not, in actuality, the world that any of us know or could reasonably endure. It is simply Thoreau's world, "a prairie for outlaws." Each one of us must seek his own way there. This is his final message, for each man is forever the eye and the Eye is the Visitor. Whatever remedy exists for life is never to be found at Walden. It exists, if at all, where the real Walden exists, somewhere in the incredible dimensions of the universal Eye.

Men esteem truth remote, in the outskirts of the system, behind the farthest star, before Adam and after the last man. In eternity there is indeed something true and sublime. But all these times and places and occasions are now and here. God himself culminates in the present moment, and will never be more divine in the lapse of all the ages.